MONEY AND TRADE CONSIDERED

With a Proposal for Supplying the Nation with Money

By

JOHN LAW

NEWTON PAGE

NEWTON PAGE

www.newtonpage.com

Money and Trade Considered
With a Proposal for Supplying the Nation with Money

By

John Law

First published by Newton Page 2013

1 3 5 7 9 10 8 6 4 2

© Newton Page 2013
All revised notes, text, headings, tables and index © Newton Page 2013
All Rights Reserved

Cover image © Newton Page 2013

ISBN 978-1-934619-06-3

Printed in the United States of America
Set in Adobe Garamond Pro

Except in the United States of America, this book is sold subject to the condition that it shall not, by way of trade or otherwise, be lent, resold, hired out, or otherwise circulated without the publisher's prior consent in any form of binding or cover than that in which it is published and without a similar condition including this condition being imposed on the subsequent purchaser.

The scanning, uploading and distribution of this book via the Internet or via any other means without the express permission of the publisher is illegal and punishable by law. Please purchase only authorized electronic editions, and do not participate in or encourage electronic piracy of copyrighted materials. Your support of both the author's and copyright holder's rights is appreciated.

NEWTON PAGE

CONTENTS

INTRODUCTION 1

CHAPTER I 5

How goods are valued—Of barter—Of silver; its value as a metal; its qualities fitting it for money; and of the additional value it received from being used as money.

CHAPTER II 13

Of trade and how far it depends on money—That the increase of the people depends on Trade—Of exchange.

CHAPTER III 33

Of the different measures which have been used to preserve and increase money—And of banks.

CHAPTER IV 41

The several measures now proposed, considered—As raising or allaying the money—Coining the plate—Regulating the balance of trade—Or, re-establishing the bank.

CHAPTER V   55

That any measures proposed for increasing the silver money or establishing a credit promising a payment of silver money are ineffectual—That silver money has fallen much from the value it had—That land is of greater value—That silver may lose the additional value it received from being used as money.

CHAPTER VI   71

The proposal given in to Parliament by Dr. H. C. examined.

CHAPTER VII   79

The proposal with reasons for it.

CHAPTER VIII   101

The low condition this country is reduced to, notwithstanding its natural advantages.

GLOSSARY   111

INTRODUCTION

INTRODUCTION

There are several proposals offer'd to remedy the difficulties the nation is under from the great scarcity of money.

That a right judgment may be made, which will be most safe, advantageous and practicable; it seems necessary, 1. That the nature of money be inquired into, and why silver was used as money preferable to other goods. 2. That trade be considered, and how far money affects trade. 3. That the measures have been used for preserving and increasing money, and these now proposed, be examined.

CHAPTER I

How goods are valued. of barter. Of silver; its value as a metal; its qualities fitting it for money; and of the additional value it received from being used as money.

CHAPTER I

Goods have a value from the uses they are applied to; and their value is greater or lesser, not so much from their more or less valuable, or necessary uses, as from the greater or lesser quantity of them in proportion to the demand for them. For example; water is of great use, yet of little value; because the quantity of water is much greater than the demand for it. Diamonds are of little use, yet of great value, because the demand for diamonds is much greater, than the quantity of them.

Goods of the same kind differ in value, from any difference in their quality, one horse is better than another horse. Barley of one country is better than barley of another country.

Goods change their value, from any change in their quantity, or in the demand for them. If oats are in greater quantity than last year, and the demand the same, or lesser, oats will be less valuable.

Mr. Locke says, the value of goods is according to their quantity in proportion to their vent. The vent of goods cannot be greater than the quantity, but the demand may be greater: if the quantity of wine brought from France be a 100 ton, and the demand be for 500 ton, the demand is greater than the vent; and the 100 ton will sell at a higher price, than if the demand were only equal to the vent. So the prices of goods are not according to the quantity in proportion to the vent, but in proportion to the demand.

Before the use of money was known, goods were exchanged by barter or contract; and contracts were made payable in goods.

This state of barter was inconvenient and disadvantageous:

1. He who desired to barter would not always find people who wanted the goods he had and had such goods as he desired in exchange.

2. Contracts taken payable in goods were uncertain, for goods of the same kind differed in value.

3. There was no measure by which the proportion of value goods had to one another could be known.

In this state of barter there was little trade and few artsmen. The people depended on the landed-men. The landed-men laboured only so much of the land as served the occasions of their families, to barter for such necessaries as their land did not produce; and to lay up for feed and bad years. What remained was unlaboured; or gifted on condition of vassalage, and other services.

The losses and difficulties that attended barter, would force the landed-men to a greater consumption of the goods of their own product, and a lesser consumption of other goods; or to supply themselves, they would turn the land to the product of the several goods they had occasion for; tho' only proper to produce of one kind. So, much of the land was unlaboured, what was laboured was not employ'd to that by which it would have turned to most advantage, nor the people to the labour they were most fit for.

Silver as a metal had a value in barter, as other goods; from the uses it was then apply'd to.

As goods of the same kind differed in value, so silver differed from silver, as it was more or less fine.

Silver was lyable to a change in its value, as other goods,

from any change in its quantity, or in the demand for it.

Silver had qualities that fitted it for the use of money:

1. It could be brought to a standard fineness, so was certain as to its quality.

2. It was easie of delivery.

3. It was of the same value in one place that it was in another; or differed little, being easie of carriage.

4. It could be kept without loss or expence; taking up little room and being durable.

5. It could be divided without loss, an ounce in four pieces, being equal in value to an ounce in one piece.

Silver, having these qualities, 'tis reasonable to think it was used as money, before it was coined. What is meant by being used as money, is, that silver in bullion was the measure by which goods were valued: the value by which goods were exchanged: and in which contracts were made payable.

He who had more goods than he had use for, would choose to barter them for silver, tho' he had no use for it; because, silver was certain in it's quality: it was easie of delivery: it could be kept without loss or expence: and with it he could purchase other goods as he had occasion, in whole or in part, at home or abroad, silver being divisible without loss, and of the same value in different places. If A. B. had 100 sheep, and desired to exchange them for horses; C. D. had 10 horses, which were equal to, or worth the 100 sheep, and was willing to exchange: but as A. B. had not present occasion for the horses, rather than be at the expence of keeping them, he would barter his sheep with E. F. who had the value to give in silver, with which he could purchase the horses at the time he had occasion.

Or if E. F. had not silver, but was satisfied to give his bond for the silver, or the horses, payable at the time A. B. wanted them; A. B. would choose to take the bond payable in silver, rather than in horses: because silver was certain in quality, and horses differed much. So silver was used as the value in which contracts were made payable.

Silver was likewise used as the measure by which goods were valued, because certain in quality. If A. B. had a 100 weight of lead, and desired to exchange it for barley, the way to know what quantity of barley was equal in value to the lead, was by the silver. If the 100 weight of lead was equal to five ounces of fine silver, and 5 ounces of fine silver equal to 20 bolls of barley, then 20 bolls was the quantity of barley to be given in exchange for the lead.

Silver being easie of carriage, so equal in one place to what it was in another; was used as the measure by which goods to be delivered in different places were valued. If a piece of wine was to be delivered at Glasgow by A. B. merchant there, to the order of C. D. merchant in Aberdeen: and the value to be delivered in oats at Aberdeen by C. D. to the order of A. B. the wine could not be valued by the quantity of oats it was worth at Glasgow, nor the oats by the quantity of wine they were worth at Aberdeen. Wine or oats might differ in quality, or be more or less valuable at the one place than at the other. The way to have known what quantity of oats was equal to the wine, was by the quantity of silver each was worth at the places they were to be delivered. If the piece of wine was worth at Glasgow 20 ounces of fine silver, and 20 ounces of fine silver worth 50 bolls of oats at Aberdeen; then 50 bolls was the quantity of oats to be given there in return for the wine.

Silver being capable of a stamp, princes, for the greater convenience of the people, set up mints to bring it to a standard, and stamp it; whereby its weight and fineness was known, without the trouble of weighing or fyning; but the stamp added nothing to the value.

For these reasons silver was used as money; its being coined was only a consequence of its being applied to that use in bullion, tho' not with the same convenience.

Mr. Locke and others who have wrote on this subject, say, the general consent of men placed an imaginary value upon silver, because of its qualities fitting it for money.[1]

I cannot conceive how different nations could agree to put an imaginary value upon any thing, especially upon silver, by which all other goods are valued; or that any one country would receive that as a value, which was not valuable equal to what it was given for; or how that imaginary value could have been kept up. But, suppose France receiving silver at an imaginary value, other nations received it at that value, because received so in France: then for the same reason a crown passing in France for 76 Sols, should pass in Scotland for 76 pence, and in Holland for 76 Stivers. But on the contrair, even in France where the crown is raised, 'tis worth no more than before when at 60 Sols.

It is reasonable to think silver was barter'd as it was valued for its uses as a mettal, and was given as money according to its value in barter. The additional use of money silver was applied to would add to its value, because as money it remedied the disadvantages and inconveniencies of barter, and consequently the demand for silver increasing, it received an additional value equal to the greater demand its use as money occasioned.

And this additional value is no more imaginary, than the value silver had in barter as a metal, for such value was because it served such uses, and was greater or lesser according to the demand for silver as a mettal, proportioned to its quantity. The additional value silver received from being used as money, was because of its qualities which fitted it for that use; and that value was according to the additional demand its use as money occasioned.

If either of these values are imaginary, then all value is so,

---

1. Locke p.31 upon interest, and p. 1. upon money.

for no goods have any value, but from the uses they are apply'd to, and according to the demand for them, in proportion to their quantity.

Thus silver having a value, and qualities fitting it for money, which other goods had not, was made money, and for the greater convenience of the people was coined.

The names of the different pieces might have been number 1. number 2. and so on; number 60 would have been the same as a crown; for the name and stamp was only to certify, that the piece had such a quantity of silver in it, of such a fineness.

Goods of any other kind that have the same qualities might then, and may now be made money equal to their value. Gold and copper may be made money, but neither with so much convenience as silver. Payments in copper being inconvenient by reason of its bulk; and gold not being in so great quantity as to serve the use of money. In countries where gold is in great quantity, it is used as money; and where gold and silver are scarce, copper is used.

Gold is coined for the more easie exchange of that metal, and copper to serve in small payments; but silver is the measure by which goods are valued, the value by which goods are exchanged, and in which contracts are made payable.

As money encreased, the disadvantages and inconveniences of barter were removed; the poor and idle were employed, more of the land was laboured, the product encreased, manufactures and trade improved, the landed-men lived better, and the people with less dependence on them.

CHAPTER II

Of Trade, and how far it depends on money. That the increase of the people depends on Trade. Of exchange.

CHAPTER II

Trade is domestick, or foreign. Domestick trade is the imployment of the people, and the exchange of goods within the country.

Foreign trade has several branches:

1. The product and manufacture being more than the consumption, a part is exported, and in return foreign goods are brought home.

2. Selling the goods exported at one port, and loading there to sell another; whereby a greater return is made, than if the goods exported had been carry'd directly there.

3. Bringing home the product and manufacture of other countries, from whence, and when they are cheap; to supply countries where, and when they are dear.

4. Bringing home the product of other countries, and exporting it in manufacture.

5. Freighting, or hireing out ships.

Domestick and foreign trade may be carried on by barter; but not for so great a value as by money, nor with so much convenience.

Domestick trade depends on the money. A greater quantity employs more people than a lesser quantity. A limited sum can only set a number of people to work proportioned to it, and 'tis with little success laws are made, for imploying the poor or idle in countries where money is scarce; good laws may bring the money to the full circulation 'tis capable of, and force it to those employments that are most profitable to the country: but no laws can make it go further, nor can more people be set to work, without more money to circulate so, as to pay the wages of a greater number. They may be brought to work on credit, and that is not practicable, unless the credit have a circulation, so as to supply the workman with necessaries; if that's supposed, then that credit is money, and will have the same effects, on home, and foreign trade.

An addition to the money adds to the value of the country. So long as money gives interest, it is imployed; and money imployed brings profit, tho' the employer loses. If 50 men are set to work, to whom 25 shillings is payed per day, and the improvement made by their labour be only equal to, or worth 15 s. yet by so much the value of the country is increased. But as it is reasonable to suppose their labour equal to 40 s. so much is added to the value of the country, of which the employer gains 15 s. 15 may be supposed to equal the consumption of the labourers, who before lived on charity, and 10 s. remains to them over their consumption.

If a stone of wooll is worth 10 s. and made into cloth worth 2 pound; the product is improved to four times the value it had in wooll: the workmen may be supposed to consume more than when they were not imployed; allow one 4th, the nation is gainer double the value of the product. So an addition to the money, whether the imployer gains or not, adds to the national wealth, eases the country of a number of poor or idle, proportioned to the money added, enables them to live better, and to bear a share in the publick with the other people.

The first branch of foreign trade, which is the export and import of goods, depends on the money. If one half of the people are imployed, and the whole product and manufacture consumed; more money, by imploying more people, will make an overplus to export: if then the goods imported ballance the goods exported, a greater addition to the money will imploy yet more people, or the same people before employed to more advantage; which by making a greater, or more valuable export, will make a ballance due. So if the money lessens, a part of the people then imployed are set idle, or imployed to less advantage; the product and manufacture is less, or less valuable, the export of consequence less, and a ballance due to foreigners.

The 2d and 3d branches of foreign trade, called the trades of carriage; are monopolized out of Europe, by these countries who have colonies; and in Europe, by these who sell cheapest.

Scotland has advantages for trade by which the merchants might undersell merchants in Holland, as cheapness of living, paying less to the publick, having workmen, seamen, and provisions for victualling cheaper: but if the Dutch merchant's stock is 10000 lib. and his yearly expence 500; he can trade at 10 per cent profit, and add yearly 500 lib. to his stock. Whereas a Scots merchant, whose stock is 500 lib. and his yearly expence 50; cannot trade so cheaply.

If 'tis asked how a Dutch merchant trades who has only 500 lib. stock? He restricts his expence so as he can afford to trade at 10 per cent profit: or money being in greater quantity in Holland, whereby it is easier borrowed, and at less use; he gets credit for more at 3 or 4 per cent, by which he gains 6 or 7. And unless money be in greater quantity in Scotland, or expence retrench'd, we cannot trade so cheap as the Dutch; tho' we have advantages for trade that they have not, and tho' they be under disadvantages we are not lyable to. By a greater quantity of money and oeconomy, the Dutch monopolize the trades of carriage even from the English.

The 4th branch of foreign trade, bringing home the

product of other countries, and exporting it in manufacture, depends on the quantity of money. We are so far from competing with the Dutch in this trade, that our wooll was sent to Holland, and imported from thence in manufacture; under the difficulty of a prohibition on the export of the wooll, and on the import of the manufacture. Yet besides the advantages already named, which we have for trade over the Dutch, the material is the product of our country, and greater privileges are granted to manufacturers here, than in Holland.

'Tis alleged, if the prohibition had continued, manufactures might have come to perfection.

The advantage some men made by manufacture, may have occasion'd the setting up of more, while the money has been diminishing; but that money so imployed, has been taken from some other use it was before imploy'd in: for money cannot serve in two places at one time.

'Tis alleged, that the allowing the wooll to be exported, occasioned the exportation of the money. That at one time 5000 lib. was sent to England to buy wooll. 'Tis askt what became of that wooll? They answer, it was sent to France for wine. Then, as 5000 lib. of English wool may be worth 8 or 10 thousand pound in France; so the 5000 lib. sent to England, saved the sending out of 8 or 10000 lib. to France.

To those who don't thoroughly examine the state of this country, it may seem odd that wooll should be allowed by law to be exported: but if the product of Scotland cannot be manufactur'd with less than 50000 people, and the money that can be spar'd to manufacture, be only capable to employ 25000, one half of the product will be lost if it is not allowed to be exported.

The 5th branch, the freighting or hireing out ships, depends on the money, and the other branches of trade. Where ships are in use to be freighted by strangers, and supported by a great demand for their own trade; there all sorts of ships are to be hired cheaper than in other places; and merchants are sure of such ships as are proper for the goods they load with, and the countries they trade to.

This trade of freighting brings the goods of other countries to Holland, tho' design'd for sale elsewhere. If woollen manufacture from England to Portugal yields 25 per cent profit, and to Holland 15; the English merchant will choose to send such goods to Holland for 15 per cent, rather than to Portugal for 25; and the Dutch merchant who is able to trade cheaper, from the cheapness of freight, etc. is satisfied for the other 10 to carry to Portugal.

Most authors who have wrote on trade divide it into national and private. They say, a merchant may gain where the nation loses. If a 1000 lib. is exported to the Indies in money or bullion, and a 1000 lib. in goods or provisions; the return worth 8000 lib. the merchant gains 6000; but as these goods are all consumed in the country, the nation loses the 1000 lib. money or bullion exported.

They don't consider whether the 8000 lib. of goods imported (all supposed to be consum'd in the country) does not lessen the consumption of the product or manufacture of the country, so as to occasion an addition to the export, at least equal to the 1000 lib. money or bullion exported. But allowing they do not lessen the consumption of the goods of the country, and the use of them be not at all necessary; yet these goods being worth 8000 lib. at home or abroad, the nation gains 6000. If the people consume them, and in extravagant uses, that's not the fault of the trade, nor for that reason should that trade be call'd disadvantageous; it is the fault of the government, who ought to hinder the too great consumption of foreign goods; especially, such as might be wanted without causing a greater consumption of the goods of the country. That care being taken, by making the vent less profitable at home, than abroad; merchants would export them, or for the future lessen the import.

If East-India goods that sell for a 1000 lib. in England, are only worth abroad 800 lib, the duty payed at their entry being return'd, and more given as a draw-back to encourage the export, their vent abroad will be more profitable than in England.

A people may consume more of their own or foreign goods, than the value of the product, manufacture, and profits by trade; but their trade is not disadvantageous, it is their too great consumption: and the too great consumption of the product and manufacture of the country, may be as hurtful as that of foreign goods; for, if so much is consumed, that the remainder exported won't pay the consumption of foreign goods, a ballance will be due, and that ballance will be sent out in money or bullion.

A nation may gain where the merchant loses, but wherever the merchant gains, the nation gains equal, and so much more, as the maintenance and wages of the people employ'd and the duty on the goods amounts to. If a ship insur'd is lost, the nation loses, and the merchant loses nothing; but in that case the insurer is the merchant, and loses equal to the nation.

As trade depends on money, so the encrease or decrease of the people depends on trade. If they have employment at home, they are kept at home: and if the trade is greater than serves to employ the people, it brings more from places where they are not employ'd. Sir William Petty values a man at 20 years purchase, by that computation a seaman whose wages is forty shil. a month, is valued at 480 lib.

Scotland has a very inconsiderable trade, because she has but a very small part of the money. There is a little home trade, but the country is not improv'd, nor the product manufactur'd.

There is a little of the first branch of foreign trade, and that is carried on with great disadvantage to the people, who pay dearer for most foreign goods, and are worse serv'd, than other nations: if they have any cheaper, 'tis from the lower duty on the import. In Scotland low prices are given for goods bought up to be exported, the merchants profit being great: if a 100 stone of wooll is worth in Holland ten piece of linen cloth, these ten pieces are sold in Scotland for the value of 180 or 200 stone of such wooll. Such goods as do not yield that great profit, are not exported; and these that do, are not exported in any quantity, the merchant's stock being small. Scotland has no part of the other branches of foreign trade, not being able to trade so cheap as other nations.

Some think if interest were lower'd by law, trade would increase, merchants being able to employ more money and trade cheaper. Such a law would have many inconveniencies, and it is much to be doubted, whether it would have any good effect; indeed, if lowness of interest were the consequence of a greater quantity of money, the stock apply'd to trade would be greater, and merchants would trade cheaper, from the easiness of borrowing and the lower interest of money, without any inconveniencies attending it.

Tho' interest were at 3 per cent in Holland, and continued at 6 in Scotland; if money were to be had equal to the demands at 6, the advantages we have for trade, which the Dutch have not, would enable us to extend trade to its other branches, notwithstanding the difference of interest.

If money in Scotland were equal to the demands at 6 per cent, the Dutch could not trade so cheap in herring; the hindrances of that trade being the consequences of the scarcity of money. The materials for carrying on the fishing are cheaper in Holland, but the cheapness of victualling alone would ballance that. And the dearth of these materials, as of other foreign goods, coming from the scarcity of money; that being remedied, these materials, and other foreign goods that are not the product of Holland, would be sold as cheap in Scotland.

Exchange, is when a merchant exports to a greater value than he imports, and has money due abroad; another importing to a greater value than he exported, has occasion for money abroad: this last by paying in money to the other, of the weight and fineness with that is due him, or to that value, saves the trouble, hazard, and expence, to himself of sending money out, to the other of bringing money home, and to both the expence of re-coyning.

So long as foreign trade, and expence kept equal, exchange was at the par: but when a people imported for a greater value, or had other occasions abroad, more than their export, and the expence of foreigners among them would ballance; there was a necessity of sending out the ballance in money or bullion, and the merchant or gentleman who owed, or had occasion for money abroad, to save the trouble, expence and hazard of sending it out, gave so much per cent to another, as the trouble, expence and hazard was valued at. Thus exchange rose above the par, and became a trade.

Mr. Mun on trade, page 100, says, the exchange being against a nation, is of advantage to that nation. And supposes, if a 100 lib. at London is worth no more than 90 lib. of the same money at Amsterdam, the Dutch to send 500000 lib. of goods to England, and the English 400000 lib. of goods to Holland; it follows, that the money due the English at Amsterdam, will ballance 440000 lib. due to the Dutch at London: so 60000 lib. pays the ballance. Mr Mun does not consider, that the Dutch goods worth 500000 lib. when exchange was at the par, are worth in London 555555 lib. when 90 lib. at Amsterdam is worth 100 lib. at London and the 400000 lib. of English goods in Holland, are only worth 360000 lib. that sum being equal by exchange to 400000 in England. So in place of England's having an advantage of 40000 lib. as he alleges by the exchange being against her: she pays 95555 lib. more, than if exchange had been at the par.

When exchange is above the par, it is not only payed for the sums due of ballance, but affects the whole exchange to the place where the ballance is due. If the balance is 20000 lib. and the sums exchanged by merchants who have money abroad, with others who are owing, or have occasion for money there, be 60000 lib. the bills for the 60000 lib. are sold at or near the same price, with the 20000 lib. of ballance.

It likewise affects the exchange to countries where no ballance is due. If the exchange betwixt Scotland and Holland is 3 per cent above the par against Scotland, betwixt England and Holland at the par, tho' no ballance is due by Scotland to England, yet the exchange with England will rise; for, a 100 lib. in England remitted to Scotland by Holland, will yield 103 lib. so betwixt Scotland and England it may be supposed to be had at 2 per cent, being less trouble than to remit by Holland.

Goods are sold to foreigners, according to the first cost. If goods worth 100 lib. in Scotland, are worth 130 lib. in England, these goods will be exported, 30 per cent being supposed enough for the charges and profit. If the price of these goods lower in Scotland from a 100 lib. to 80, the price in England will not continue at 130; it will lower proportionably, for either Scots merchants will undersell one another, or English merchants will export these goods themselves. So if they rise in Scotland from a 100 lib. to 120; they will rise proportionably in England, unless the English can be served with these goods cheaper from other places, or can supply the use of them with goods of another kind. This being supposed, it follows that, by so much as exchange is above the par, so much all goods exported are sold cheaper, and all goods imported are sold dearer than before. If a merchant send goods yearly to England first cost, charges and profit 6000 lib. money in England of the same standard with money in Scotland, and no ballance due; but a ballance due to Holland, raising the exchange 3 per cent above the par to Holland, and affecting the exchange to England 2 per cent, 5882 lib. 7 sh. in England pays the goods, that sum by exchange being equal to 6000 lib. in Scotland. So that a ballance due to Holland, by raising the exchange to other countries, occasions a loss to Scotland of 117 lib. 13 sh. on the value of 6000 lib. of goods sent to England.

English goods are sold so much dearer. If an English merchant sends goods yearly to Scotland, first cost, charges and profit 6000 lib. 6120 lib. must be payed for these goods in Scotland, being only equal to 6000 lib. in England. If the exchange had been at the par, the Scots goods sent to England would have sold 117 lib. and 14 sh. more, and the English goods sent to Scotland 120 lib. less.

Thus to all places with whom exchange is above the par, goods sent out are sold so much less, and goods brought from thence are sold so much dearer, as the exchange is above the par; whether sent out, or brought in, by Scots or foreign merchants.

The merchant who deals in English goods gains no more than when exchange was at the par, tho' he sells dearer; nor the merchant who deals in Scots goods less, tho' he sells cheaper; they have both the same profit as when exchange was at the par. Scotland pays 2 per cent more for English goods, and England 2 per cent less for Scots goods: all, or a great part of the loss falls at last on the landed man in Scotland, and it is the landed man in England has all, or a great part of the benefit.

Nations finding the export of money or bullion to pay the ballance due by trade, a loss of so much riches, and very hurtful to trade, might have discharged the import of such goods as the people could best want; or laid a duty on them, such as might have lessen'd their consumption: they might have given encouragement to industry, whereby the product would have been increas'd and improv'd, or discouraged extravagant consumption, whereby the overplus to export would have been greater; any one of these methods would have brought trade and exchange equal, and have made a ballance due them: but in place of these measures, they prohibit bullion and money to be exported, which could not well have any other effect, than to raise the exchange equal to the hazard, such laws added to the export of money or bullion, which may be supposed 3 per cent more: and as these laws by such effect were hurtful, making all goods exported sell yet 3 per cent cheaper, and all goods imported 3 per cent dearer; the stricter they were execute, the higher the exchange rose, and the more they did hurt. The ballance was still sent out in money or bullion, by the merchant who owed it, by the banker who gave the bills, or by the foreigner to whom it was due.

Suppose the money of Scotland, England, and Holland of the same weight and fineness. Scotland to trade with no other places. The exchange at the par. The yearly export from Scotland, first cost 300000 lib. charges and profit 30 per cent. Goods imported 280000 lib. Charges and profit 30 per cent. One half of the trade to be carried on by Scots merchants, the other half by English and Dutch.

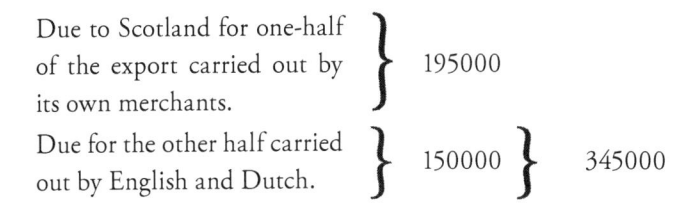

Due to Scotland for one-half of the export carried out by its own merchants.	195000	
Due for the other half carried out by English and Dutch.	150000	345000

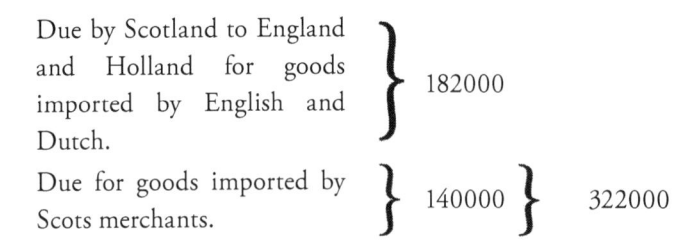

Due by Scotland to England and Holland for goods imported by English and Dutch. } 182000

Due for goods imported by Scots merchants. } 140000 } 322000

The expence of Scots-men abroad, more than of foreigners in Scotland, 40000 lib. If this is supposed the yearly state of the trade and expence of Scotland, there will be a ballance due of 17000 lib. and unless the Scots retrench the consumption of foreign goods, so as to import less; or retrench the consumption of their own goods, so as to export more; or increase, or improve their product, so as the export be greater or more valuable; or retrench in their expence abroad. Since that ballance must be paid it will go out in money or bullion: and occasions the exchange to rise 3 per cent, the prohibition on the export of money 3 more, if Scots-men export it, the Nation saves 1020 lib. exchange on the 17000 of ballance due, which is lost if English merchants export it; but the loss such a rise in exchange occasions on the goods, is more considerable. The 195000 lib. due abroad for goods sent out of Scotland by Scots merchants, will be payed with 183962 lib. English or Dutch money, that sum being equal by exchange at 6 per cent to 195000 lib. in Scotland. The 150000 lib. due for first cost of goods carried out by English or Dutch merchants, will be payed with 141510 lib. English or Dutch money, that sum being equal to 150000 lib. in Scotland. The 182000 lib. due by Scotland for goods imported by English and Dutch merchants, will come to 192920 lib. in Scotland. And the 140000 lib. first cost of goods brought home by Scots merchants, will come to 148400 lib. in Scotland. So the accompt will run thus:

Due to Scotland for goods exported.	183962
Brought from abroad first cost.	140000
Balance of expence abroad.	40000
Due to Scotland abroad.	3962
Due by Scotland for goods imported by English and Dutch.	192920
English and Dutch take back in goods.	150000
Due to English and Dutch in Scotland.	42920
3962 lib. due abroad to Scotland in Scots money.	4199
Remains due by Scotland.	38721

So the rise in the exchange of 3 per cent by the ballance due of 17000 lib. and 3 more by the prohibition on the export of money, occasions a loss to Scotland of 21721 lib. and makes the next year's ballance 38721 lib. tho' the trade be the same as before. Of which 21721 lib. lost by exchange, one half would be saved if money were allowed to be exported.

Since the exchange being 6 per cent above the par, occasions the loss of 21721 lib. then raising the money 8 and a one third per cent, having raised the exchange with England to 14 per cent, and with Holland to 30 per cent, makes the loss proportionably greater: Scots goods being supposed to continue at the same prices they were sold for, before the money was raised, or not to rise in the same proportion with the money. For when exchange was at the par, a 100 lib. of Scots goods were sold abroad for a 130 lib. English money; but 114 lib.

English money, being now equal by exchange to a 130 lib. in Scotland, the Scots merchant can afford to sell the same quantity of goods for a 114 lib. that he sold before at a 130, and have the same profit. So foreign goods worth abroad a 100 lib. and sold in Scotland for a 130 lib. when exchange was at the par; cannot be sold now for less than a 150 lib. in Scotland, that sum being only equal to a 130 lib. English money; and the merchant's profit is no greater, than when he sold the same quantity of goods for a 130 lib.

It may not be improper to consider what consequences would attend the lowering the money to the English standard, and allowing it to be exported.

The former state of trade I have supposed to be carried on, one half by Scots merchants, the other half by English and Dutch; but, as most of the trade is carried on by Scots merchants, I shall suppose this state of trade accordingly. The one or the other will clear the matter in question.

The state of trade now, and exchange supposed at 15 per cent to England, and 30 to Holland. The whole export of Scotland to be 300000 lib. of which 250000 lib. carried out by Scots merchants, sold at 30 per cent profit and charges 325000 lib.

In English money.	282608
Exported by foreigners for 50000 lib. in English money.	43478
The whole export.	326086
Goods imported.	306086
Spent abroad.	40000
Due of ballance by Scotland.	20000

Money being lowered to the English standard, and allowed by law to be exported; will bring the exchange with England to 2 per cent or 3 per cent, and with Holland to 17 per cent or 18 per cent, notwithstanding of the balance due. For, as £100 in Edinburgh, would then be equal to £100 at London, and being allowed to be exported; none would give above £102, or 3 per cent here for £100 at London: because the trouble and charge of sending it to London, would be valued no higher, the export, import, and expence abroad supposed to continue the same; a balance would then be due to Scotland.

The state of trade, exchange at 3 per cent to England, and proportionately to other places.

Due in English money, for 325000 lib. first cost, charges and profit of goods sent out by Scots merchants.	315534
Due in English money for 50000 lib. of goods exported by foreigners.	48544
The whole export.	364078
Of this deduce the value of goods imported.	306086
And also the expence abroad.	40000
There will be a ballance due to Scotland, of	17992

As this ballance due to Scotland, would bring exchange to the par, and 3 per cent on the Scots side; 3 more because money in England is prohibited to be exported; 100 lib. in Scotland, would be worth 106 lib. in England, and proportionably in other places. So the state of trade would then be thus:

Due in English money for 325000 lib. first cost, charges and profit of Scots goods sent out by Scots merchants, and 50000 lib. exported by foreigners.	397500
Of this spent abroad.	40000
Imported from abroad.	306086
Ballance then due to Scotland.	51414

If the yearly export be as great as I suppose it, and the ballance only 20000 pounds; then lowering the money to the English standard, will make a ballance due of 51414 lib. tho' the money is not allowed to be exported.

It may be objected, that such an alteration in the exchange, lowering the value of foreign money; might hinder the sale of our goods abroad. For, linen-cloth bought in Scotland for 100 lib. and sold in London for a 115 lib. yields by exchange 31 per cent profit. But if exchange were 6 per cent on the Scots side, the profit is only 9 per cent.

It is answered. If an English merchant takes bills on Scotland for a 1000 lib. to lay out on linen-cloth, the exchange then at the par: the linen-cloth is sold in England according to the first cost, charges and usual profit. Next year the exchange is on the English side, the linen is sold in England cheaper than before. The third year exchange returns to the par, the linen is then sold in England as the first year. If the first cost of linen is dearer, the consumer pays the more for it, the merchant's profit is the same.

All nations endeavour to get the exchange as much as they can on their side. The exchange from Holland to England is 12 or 15 per cent, to Scotland 30 per cent, to France 40 or 50, sometimes more; yet Dutch goods sell in these countries, the merchant has his profit the same as when exchange was lower, the consumer pays more for them. English cloth is sold at Paris from 18 to 20 livres the French ell when the lued'ore is at 12 livres, from 20 to 23, when the lued'ore is at 14 livres: because the exchange to England is dearer, in proportion as the French money is rais'd.

Most goods sent from Scotland are such as foreigners won't want, tho' they payed 10 or 20 per cent more for them. We have an example of this in the wooll. During the prohibition, wooll sold in Holland and France for double the first cost, now it has fallen to 30 or 40 per cent profit. Prices are given for goods according to their first cost, charges, and usual profit; where prohibitions are, the hazard of exporting contrair to law is valued. Wooll is of less value now in Holland than in time of peace, because the vent of their woollen manufacture is less; but tho' wool were as valuable in Holland as before, and tho' a Dutch manufacturer would give 200 lib. for wooll that cost only a 100 lib. in Scotland, rather than want it: yet as he knows the prohibition is taken off, and that the Scots merchants can afford to sell cheaper; he won't buy unless he can have it at a reasonable profit. So either the Scots merchants bring down the price, by underselling one another; or the Dutch merchant commissions it himself. If a duty were put on such goods whose value abroad would bear it, the merchant would gain the same, 'tis the foreigner pays the duty.

Besides, lowering the money may not lower the prices abroad. For, as when money was raised, goods may have rose in proportion, or have been made worse; so as a 100 lib. after the money is lower'd will have 33 crowns and one sixth more silver in it, than a 100 lib. had before; so a greater quantity of goods may be bought with a 100 lib. than before, or the goods may be made better: especially the linen-cloth, since the material would be imported for less. But, allowing that upon the lowering the money, goods sold in Scotland as before, and were made no better; and allowing that one third or more of the goods exported, could not be raised in their prices abroad; because foreigners might be served cheaper with the same kind of goods from other places, or might supply the use of them with goods of another kind; or might consume less of them; yet, that ought not to hinder such a regulation of the money and exchange; for a draw-back might be given upon the export of such goods, whose prices abroad were not great enough to yield a reasonable profit.

But lest such an alteration in the exchange, or undervaluing foreign money, should lessen the export of goods: it may not be advisable, unless a fund were given, out of which draw-backs might be payed to encourage export, and an addition be made to the money, whereby the people may be set to work. For without some addition to the money, 'tis not to be supposed next year's export can be equal to the last: it will lessen as money has lessened; a part of the people then imployed being now idle; not for want of inclination to work, or for want of imployers, but for want of money to imploy them with.

CHAPTER III

Of the different measures which have been used to preserve and increase money. And of banks.

CHAPTER III

The measures which have been used to preserve and increase money, have in some countries been opposite to what has been used in others: and opposite measures have been used in the same countries, without any differing circumstances to occasion them.

Some countries have raised money in the denomination, when others have lowered it; some have allay'd it, when others who had allay'd it have rectified it; some have prohibited the export of money under fevered penalties, when others have by law allowed it to be exported; some thinking to add to the money, have obliged traders to bring home bullion, in proportion to the goods they imported. Most countries have tryed some or all of these measures, and others of the same nature, and have tryed contrary measures at one time, from what they used immediately before, from the opinion, that since the method used had not the effect designed, a contrary would: yet it has not been found, that any of them have preserved or increased money; but on the contrair.

The use of banks has been the best method yet practiced for the increase of money. Banks have been long used in Italy, but as I am informed, the invention of them was owing to Sweedland. Their money was copper, which was inconvenient, by reason of its weight and bulk; to remedy this inconveniency, a bank was set up where the money might be pledged, and credit given to the value, which past in payments, and facilitate trade.

The Dutch for the same reason set up the bank of Amsterdam. Their money was silver, but their trade was so great as to find payments even in silver inconvenient. This bank like that of Sweedland, is a secure place, where merchants may give in money, and have credit to trade with. Besides the convenience of easier and quicker payments, these banks save the expence of casheers, the expence of bags and carriage, losses by bad money, and the money is safer than in the merchants houses, for 'tis less lyable to fire or robbery, the necessary measures being taken to prevent them.

Merchants who have money in the bank of Amsterdam, and people of other countries who deal with them, are not lyable to the changes in the money, by its being allay'd or altered in the denomination: for the bank receives no money but what's of value, and is therefore called bank-money; and tho' raised in current payments, it goes for the value it was pledged for in bank-payments. The agio of the bank changes a quarter or a half per cent, as current money is more or less scarce.

Banks where the money is pledg'd equal to the credit given, are sure; for tho' demands are made of the whole, the bank does not fail in payment.

By the constitution of this bank, the whole sum for which credit is given, ought to remain there, to be ready at demand; yet a sum is lent by the managers for a stock to the lumbar, and 'tis thought they lend great sums on other occasions. So far as they lend they add to the money, which brings a profit to the country, by imploying more people, and extending trade; they add to the money to be lent, whereby it is easier borrowed, and at less use; and the bank has a benefit: but the bank is less sure, and tho' none suffer by it, or are apprehensive of danger, its credit being good; yet if the whole demands were made, or demands greater than the remaining money, they could not all be satisfied, till the bank had called in what sums were lent.

The certain good it does, will more than ballance the hazard, tho' once in two or three years it failed in payment; providing the sums lent be well secured: merchants who had money there, might be disappointed of it at demand, but the security being good, and interest allowed; money would be had on a small discount, perhaps at the par.

Last war, England set up a bank to have the conveniences of that at Amsterdam, and by their constitution to increase money. This bank was made up of subscribers who lent the King 1200000 lib. at 8 and a third per cent, for 11 years, on a parliamentary fund; and were privileged bankers for that time. The sum due by the government was a security to the people, to make good any losses the bank might suffer.

This bank was safer than the goldsmiths' notes in use before. It made a great addition to the money, having a much greater sum of notes out, than money in bank. And the sum lent the King, which was the fund belonged to the subscribers, was negotiated at profit, and had the same effect in trade as money. I don't know how their notes came to be at discount, whether from the circumstances of the nation, or from ill management.

The fund of the bank of Scotland was 100000 lib. of which a tenth was payed in. This bank was safer than that of England, there being a register whereby most sums lent were secured. Its notes went for 4 or 5 times the value of the money in bank, and by so much as these notes went for more than the money in bank; so much was added to the money of the nation.

This bank was more useful than that of Amsterdam, or England; its notes passing in most payments, and through the whole country: the bank of Amsterdam being only for that town, and that of England of little use but at London.

The stop of payments that happened to the bank of Scotland, was foreseen, and might have been prevented. The consumption of foreign goods and expence in England, being more than the export of goods did pay; the ballance sent out in money lessened the credit of the bank. For, as credit is voluntary, it depends on the quantity of money in the country, and increases or decreases with it. Coyning notes of one pound supported the bank, by furnishing paper for small payments, and thereby preventing a part of the demand for money: by these notes the bank might have kept its credit, till other methods had been taken to supply the country with money; had not a report of raising the money occasioned an extraordinary demand, which in few days exhausted the money in bank, and put a stop to payments.

It would not have been easie in that scarcity of money to have got enough to support the bank, tho' men of the best credit had undertaken it; that report of raising the money having only occasioned a demand from the people in Edinburgh. In a short time notes would have come in so fast from the country, that what money could have been got, would not have answered the demand.

If the Privy Council had lowered the money, the English crown to 5 s. and the other money in proportion, to take place 2 pence p. crown in 3 days, and the other 3 pence in a month; the occasion of the demand being removed, in all appearance money would have been returned to the bank.

If the state of the bank had been known, or suspected by the people; such a proclamation would have had the same effect, tho' the stop of payment had then happen'd. In that case, the support of the bank might have been the narrative of the proclamation; the security being good, few or none would have kept their money to loss, rather than return it to the bank. And if in 3 days money had not come in so fast as expected, their lordships, by a 2d. proclamation, might have lowered the crown to 5 sh. to take place then, and 6 pence more in 3 days. When the credit of the bank had been re-established, the money might have been cryed up, if that had been necessary, the crown to 5 sh. and 5 pence, and the other money in proportion as it was before.

Some are against all banks where the money does not lie pledged equal to the credit. First, they say the demand may be greater than the money in the bank. Secondly, if we are declining in our trade, or money, we are not at all, or are less sensible of it: and if the bank fails, we are in a worse condition than before.

To the first it's answered. Tho' the nation had no benefit by the addition the bank makes to the money; nor the people by being supply'd with money when otherwise they could not, and at less interest; and tho' the proprietors had no gain by it: the other conveniences, as quicker and easier payments, &c. are more than equal to that hazard; or bank notes, gold-smiths and bankers notes, would not be preferred to money, every body knowing such a stop may happen to the bank, and that gold-smiths and bankers may fail.

The other objection is the same as to say, a merchant who had a small stock, and was capable of imploying a greater; if a sum were offered him without interest, equal to what he had, and more as his own increased, should refuse it, because he might fancy himself richer than he was, and if his own stock decreased, that sum lent would be taken from him.

If 15000 is supposed the money in bank, and 75000 lib. of notes out; 60000 lib. is added to the money of the nation, without interest: for what is payed by the borrowers, is got by the proprietors. As the money of the nation increases, the credit of the bank increases, and the sum of notes out is greater; and so far from making the people less sensible of the condition of the country, a surer judgment of the state of trade and money may be made from the books of the bank, than any other way.

If trade can be carried on with 100000 lib. and a ballance then due by foreigners; the same measures and a greater quantity of money, would make the ballance greater. Nor is that additional money the bank furnishes, to be supposed will be lost, if by a ballance due from trade the silver money increases: that credit may fail from an accident when money is plentiful, and would soon be recovered; 'tis only lost by a scarcity of money. Such a credit may support trade, in cases where without it trade would sink, but cannot do prejudice.

Another objection is made against the bank. That it encouraged the exportation of money by furnishing sums in such species as were of most value abroad. To answer this objection, I shall make a supposition. A. B. merchant has occasion for 1000 lib. in Holland, and desires C. D. banker to give him a bill for that value; there is no money due in Holland to Scots merchants, so C. D. must export the money to pay the bill he draws: but, there being no bank, nor any possibility of getting 1000 lib. in 40 pence pieces, he sends out money of different species. This does not hinder the money to go out, but makes the exchange dearer by 2 or 3 per cent, than it would have been if 40 pence pieces could have been got. And tho' no other money were left, but old marks, if a ballance is due, these will go out, tho' not worth 10 pence: the exchange will be so much higher, the profit of exporting is the same; and so far from doing hurt to the country, the bank by furnishing such pieces as could be exported to least loss, kept the exchange 2 or 3 per cent lower than otherwise it would have been, and saved yearly the sending out a considerable sum to pay a greater ballance, the higher exchange would have occasioned.

CHAPTER IV

The several measures now proposed, considered. As raising or allaying the money. Coyning the plate. Regulating the ballance of trade. Or, re-establishing the bank.

CHAPTER IV

When I use the words, raising the money, I desire to be understood raising it in the denomination; for I do not suppose it adds to the value.

There is no way silver can be made more valuable, but by lessening the quantity, or increasing the demand for it. If the export and consumption of silver be greater than the import, or the demand be increased; silver will be of more value. If the quantity imported be greater than the quantity exported or consumed, or the demand lessened; silver will be of less value.

If raising or allaying the money could add to its value, or have any good effect on home or foreign trade; then no nation would want money. A 100 lib. might be raised or allayed to 2, to 10, to a 100 times the denomination it had, or more as there were occasion. But as 'tis unjust to raise, or allay money; because, then all contracts are payed with a lesser value than was contracted for; and as it has bad effects on home or foreign trade: so no nation practices it, that has regard to justice, or understands the nature of trade and money. If A. B. sell 12 chalder of victual for a 100 lib. payable in 6 months, with which he is to pay bills of exchange of that value, to be drawn on him then from France for wine he has commission'd; and in that time the money is raised or allayed to double, the 100 lib. A. B. receives will only pay half of the bill he has to pay, being only equal to 50 lib. of the money he contracted for. Nor will that 100 lib. buy the same quantity of goods of the country, that a 100 lib. bought before: it will pay where money is due, and satisfie past contracts made upon the faith of the publick, because the prince says every man shall take half what is owing him in full payment. But in bargains to be made, the value of the money will be considered; goods will rise, tho' perhaps not to the proportion the money is raised; and such persons as do not raise their goods, equal to the money, are imposed on.

When 6 pence is raised to 12 pence, the 6 pence is worth 12 pence, but the value of the pence is lowered to half-pence.

To explain this matter better, I shall suppose when money is raised, goods rise, or not.

If goods rise, then raising the money has not the effect designed. If a piece of serge is sold for 40 sh. and the shilling be raised to 18 pence, the piece of serge will be sold for 3 lib. This adds to the tale of the money, and pays debts with two thirds of what is due, but does not add to the money. This is the natural consequence of raising the money; for, it is not the sound of the higher denomination, but the value of the silver is considered.

If, when money is raised, goods keep the prices they had before: then all goods exported are sold for a lesser value abroad, and all goods imported are sold dearer. A half-crown is raised to 40 pence, and that half-crown buys the same quantity of goods 40 pence bought before; then the merchant who sends goods to Holland, to the value of 300 lib. which are sold for 390 lib. there, would gain 220 lib. on the value of 300 lib. exported: because, 390 lib. in Holland, would be equal to, or worth by exchange at the par, or sent in bullion, 520 lib. in Scotland. That trade would bring no more profit to the nation, than when the return of the goods yielded only 390 lib. for, 390 lib. before it was raised, had the same quantity of silver, that 520 lib. rais'd money would have; and bought as great a quantity of foreign goods. But that trade would be so profitable to the merchant, that more people would deal in it than could get goods to buy; and as more buyers than sellers would raise the prices here, so one merchant underselling the other would lower the prices in Holland. But tho' the prices kept low here, and our merchants kept up the prices abroad: the Dutch knowing the goods were so cheap in the country, would buy none from our merchants, but commission them in return of goods they sent.

Suppose the yearly export first cost 300000 lib. sold abroad 390000 lib. The import, and expence abroad 410000 lib. and 20000 lib. sent in money to pay the ballance. The money raised one third, and goods to keep the prices they had before, 225000 lib. sent to Scotland in foreign money, or goods, or by exchange, would buy what was sold abroad for 390000 lib. The export, import, and expence abroad continuing the same, Scotland would be due a ballance of 185000 lib. For, tho' Scots goods were sold under the value, yet other nations would not sell their goods for less than before; or than they could have in other places.

It may be alledged, we have more product and manufacture, than is consumed or exported; and selling cheaper, would occasion a greater demand for our goods abroad.

The product and manufacture might be much increased, if we had money to employ the people: but, I'm of the opinion we have not any great quantity of goods, more than what is consumed or exported. Allow selling cheaper would occasion a greater demand; that the greater demand, would occasion an increase in the product, and manufacture, to the value of 100000 lib. and allow that the extraordinary cheapness of goods, did not occasion a greater consumption in the country: yet, we would be in the same condition as before; 20000 lib. would be still due of ballance, and the improvement would be given to foreigners for nothing. But this improvement is imaginary, for tho' the demand increased, yet without more money more people could not be imployed, so no further improvement could be made: we would be forced to retrench near one half of the ordinary consumption of foreign goods, and expence abroad; not having money to pay the great ballance would be due.

Some think foreign money being raised, would bring in money to Scotland.

Tho' the crown were raised to 10 s. yet if a ballance is due by Scotland, the exchange will be above the par, and, 'tis not to be supposed an English merchant will bring crowns to Scotland, when for a 100 crowns payed in at London, he can have 105 or 6 of the same crowns payed him at Edinburgh.

If the ballance of trade was equal, foreign money raised, and Scots money not raised, in proportion; foreign money would be brought in, and a greater value of Scots money would be carried out. 'Tis the same loss to a country when money is raised, and goods do not rise in proportion: if foreigners send in money to buy goods, and this money when exported is not valued so high as here; the return in goods will be so much less, besides the want of the profit we would have had on the export of our goods.

If all import and foreign expence were discharged, Scotland would then be so much richer, as there was bullion or money imported: but, if that prohibition be supposed, Scotland would be richer by keeping the money at the value it has; because a greater quantity would be brought in, to buy the same quantity of goods.

If we could be supposed to be without any commerce with other nations, a 100 lib. may be allayed and raised to have the same effect in trade as a million: but, if a stranger were suffered to come to Scotland, he might purchase a great part of the land or goods with a small sum. And a rich man here would make a very small figure abroad.

Money is the measure by which all goods are valued; and unless goods rise to the full proportion the money is raised, the goods are undervalued. If the yearly value of Scotland in product and manufacture be 2 millions, at 20 years purchase 40 millions. The money a 100000 lib. Raising the money a 20 per cent, makes it pass for 120000 lib. Suppose the goods rise only 10 per cent, then that a 120000 lib. is equal in Scotland to a 110000 lib. of the money before it was raised; and buys the same quantity of goods. So, an addition is made of 20000 lib. to the tale and of 10000 lib. to the value of Scots or foreign money, compared with the value of Scots goods: but the measure by which goods are valued, being raised in the denomination 20 per cent; and the goods rising only 10 per cent: Scotland is near 4 million, or one tenth less valuable than before. And any man who sells his estate, will receive a tenth less silver, or of any other foreign goods for it, than if he had sold it before the money was raised.

France and Holland are given as examples of raising and allaying the money. In France the money is higher in the denomination than in other countries, but that does not hinder the money of France to be exported. When the lued'ore was at 12 livres, the ballance was against France, exchange 10 per cent above the par: and a 110 lued'ores at 12 livres were payed then at Paris, for a 100 lued'ores of the same weight and fineness at Amsterdam, and passing there for 9 guilders bank money; so 10 per cent was got by exporting money from France. When the lued'ore was raised to 14 livres, that did not make the ballance against France less; the exchange continued the same, 110 lued'ores tho' at 14 livres were payed for a bill of a 100 at Amsterdam, and the same profit was made by exporting money. If the exchange happened to be lower, it was from the ballance of trade due by France being less, and that would have lowered the exchange whether the money had been raised or not. But the raising the money, so far from bringing the ballance to the French side, keeps the ballance against France: for, as their goods do not rise to the full proportion the money is raised, so French goods are sold cheaper, and foreign goods are sold dearer, which makes the ballance greater, occasions a greater export of money, sets idle so many of the people as that money employed, lessens the product or manufacture, the yearly value of the country, and the number of the people.

It is thought the Dutch coin lued'ores, and send them to France, where they pass at 14 livres. And, that guineas were sent from Holland to England, in the time of the clipt money; because they past there for 30 s. But these people are misinformed. Ever since I have known any thing of exchange, a lued'ore at Amsterdam whether new or old, has been of more value by exchange, than a new lued'ore at Paris. And in the time of the clipt money, a guinea in Holland was worth more by exchange, than a guinea in England. These who were ignorant of the exchange, might buy up guineas or lued'ores, to carry to England or France, but they would have got more by bill. There was a profit then upon exporting guineas and lued'ores from England and France to Holland. The pound English at that time was given for 8 guilders, or under; and the exchange from Amsterdam to Paris has been these 8 or 10 years for the most part, considerably above the par on the Dutch side. I have known the pound English at 7 guilders 13 stivers, and the French crown of 3 livres bought in Holland for 37 stivers, in London for 39 pence half penny.

Raising the money in France is laying a tax on the people, which is sooner payed, and thought to be less felt than a tax laid on any other way. When the King raises the lued'ore from 12 livres to 14, they are taken in at the mint for 13 livres, and given out for 14 livres; so the King gains a livre on the lued'ore, and this tax comes to 20 or 25 million of livres, sometimes more, according to the quantity of money in the country. But so far from adding to the money, it stops the circulation: a part being kept up till there is occasion to export it to Holland, from whence a return is made by bill, of a sum of livres equal to the same quantity of new lued'ores that were exported of old ones, and 8 or 10 per cent more, according as the exchange is on the Dutch side. Others who won't venture to send the money out, keep it till the new money is cryed down, so save a 13th part, which the King would have got if they had carried the money to the mint to be recoined. This tax falls heavy on the poorer sort of the people.

'Tis generally thought the Dutch money is not worth half what it passes for. But it will prove otherwise when examined. The bank by which most payments are made, receive and pay in bank money, which is better than the English, ducatdowns are at 3 guilders, and other bank money in proportion; and I'm informed the current money has silver in it to the value or near, except some of their skellings which are worse than others: the making them worse was not design'd, it was an abuse occasioned by too many towns having power to coin: which abuse was stopped so soon as known, and that species cryed down to 5 stivers and a half.

Some propose the money may be raised, to give the little we have left a better circulation, and to bring out hoarded money. The lowering it by degrees to take place in 3 or 4 months, will have the same effect; and other good consequences: for, from what has been said, page 28 and 29.[1] There is reason to think, if the money were lowered to the English standard, exchange would be on our side, and a ballance due us: providing the export, the import, and expence abroad continued as now.

There is another argument for raising the money, which

---

1. Pages 54 and 55 of the 1750 edition.

is, that some goods don't yield profit enough abroad, so are not exported. If serges worth in Scotland a 100 lib. are worth 120 in Holland, the merchant won't export them for 20 per cent profit: but if the money is raised 20 per cent, and goods keep at the prices they had before, the same money that bought 100 lib. of serges, buying now to the value of 120 lib. and these goods being worth in Holland 144 lib: that addition to the profit by raising the money, will occasion the export of them.

This is the same as if a merchant who had a 100 different sorts of goods, and was offered 30 per cent profit upon 90 of them; but no body offering above 20 per cent profit for the other 10 sorts, should add a quarter to the measure by which he measured his goods, and sell all the 100 sorts for the same price he sold them before: as this merchant would find himself a considerable loser by this expedient, so will a nation who raises their money.

For the same reason, it would be a great loss to Scotland if all goods were allowed to be exported without duty; some ought to be free of duty, and some not, according to their value abroad.

The true and safe way to encourage the export of such goods, as do not yield great enough profit; is by a draw-back. If serges sent to Holland give only 20 per cent profit, 10 per cent given as a draw-back will encourage their export: the draw-back given to the merchant is not lost to the nation, and what is got by the manufacture or export of the goods, is gained by the nation.

A draw-back is the best method yet known for encouraging trade, and it may be made appear, that 10 or 15000 applyed that way, will occasion an addition to the export to the value of 100000 lib. Nor is any part of that 10 or 15000 lib. lost to the nation; for, if A. B. and C. Scotsmen get such draw-back, it is the same thing to the nation, as if it had not been given.

When draw-backs are paid out of funds for the support of the government, little money is applyed that way; because, so much is taken from the prince: but, if there was a national fund for the encouragement of trade, that nation might improve trade, and undersell other nations that did not follow the same measures. But this is supposing there was money in the country to imploy the people.

Coining the plate were a loss of the fashion, which may be valued one 6th, and would add little to the money: the plate at the restauration was inconsiderable, having been called in a little before. Since there may have been wrought one year with another about 60 stone weight; of that a great part has been melted down, or exported, the remainder won't be of great value. What plate has been imported belongs to a few men of quality, who will send it out of the country rather than lose the fashion; and in that they do a service to the country, providing they don't spend it abroad, because wrought plate will sell for more silver at London, than it will melt to here.

If 'tis proposed the money be allayed, and the advantage of the allay be given to the owners of the plate. Suppose the new money with allay be raised to double the denomination; 5 sh. of plate with the fashion worth 6 sh. will give at the mint 10 sh. allay'd money: but even then the plate will not be brought in voluntarily, for that plate sold in England, and the value brought back by bill, will yield from 11 to 12 sh. Exchange being above the par, and 6 pence supposed to be got for the fashion of the ounce of plate.

If it be necessary to coin the plate, such plate should be allowed to be exported as can be sold abroad for more than its weight: security being given to import money or bullion to the value.

Some propose a regulation of the ballance of trade, by retrenching the consumption of foreign goods, and expence in England: so the ballance being brought to be on our side, we may become rich by living within our yearly value, as we became poor by spending beyond it.

Such a regulation will have its difficulties: 1. To discharge all or a great part of the import, will lessen considerably the revenue of the Crown; and her majesty may not think good to give the royal ascent to such a regulation, unless an equivalent be given. 2. Such a regulation would not be so strictly kept, but a part of what was used to be imported would be stole in. 3. The residence of our princes being in England, we are under a necessity of having a ministry there: imployments being at the disposal of the prince, and London being a place of more diversion than Edinburgh, the gentry will continue to go to London for places or pleasure.

But allowing the royal ascent were given to such a regulation; either with or without an equivalent; and the regulation could be so strictly kept, that nothing were imported contrair to that law; and allow 20000 lib. could be saved of the expence in England, so that the import and expence abroad should be 60000 lib. less than last year: yet there are other difficulties, that I fear will make the regulation ineffectual:

1. Suppose the ballance last year due by us was 20000 lib. the import and expence abroad lessened 60000 lib. These who propose this regulation may think a ballance will be due to us of 40000 lib. But as the bank may have supplyed us with 60000 lib. of notes, more than the money in bank: and as 20000 lib. is supposed to have been exported last year: so our money being lessened 80000 lib. the next year's export may be so much less valuable, the want of that money having set idle a part of the people were then imployed: and a greater ballance be due than last year, notwithstanding of the regulation.

2. 40000 lib. first cost of goods imported, and 20000 lib. spent abroad, lessened the consumption of the goods of

the country; and the export was by so much greater, as the consumption of the goods of the country was lessened. But this regulation occasioning a greater consumption of the goods of the country, the export will be less.

3. Several merchants may have exported goods, tho' they had not much profit upon the export of them; but because of the profit to be made upon the import; which being lessen'd, may likewise lessen the export.

4. If Scotland discharge or put a very high duty on the goods of other nations, other nations may discharge Scots goods.

Allowing there were no difficulties in regulating the ballance of trade, and that the same measures were followed as are followed in Holland; we would grow richer, but their riches would increase in the same proportion: and 50 years hence Scotland would be as poor as now, in comparison with Holland.

If two countries equal in their product, people, &c. the one with a 100000 lib. of money, and living within its yearly value; so that the first year a ballance is due of 20000 lib. the second year of 25000 lib. and so on. The other country with 20 millions of money, and consuming more than the yearly value; so that a million is sent out to pay the ballance, the second year 1200000 lib. and so on. This country will be soon poor, and the other will be soon rich: but if that people who has 20 millions of money, will retrench in proportion to the other; they will be rich and powerful in comparison with the other.

Considering how small a share we have of the money of Europe, and how much trade depends on money: it will not be found very practicable to better our condition, but by an addition to our money. Or if it is practicable without it, it is much more so with it.

The bank will add little to the money; for as credit is

voluntary, it depends on the quantity of money in the country. And tho' the bank had never failed, yet it could not have kept its credit much longer. Because, the quantity of money in Scotland is not sufficient to give a circulation to such a sum of notes, as will pay the charges of the bank, and the interest to the owners.

'Tis thought the proprietors of the bank design to apply to the parliament for further priviledges: but as their design is not yet made publick, I shall only say in general, that if other priviledges are to be given, then it is not the same bank; at least not on the same establishment it was: in either of these cases, every person should be allowed to share in it.

When a bank is establish'd every person may have a share, upon the terms of the act of parliament; and he that offers first is preferred. Suppose upon the setting up of the bank, A. B. and C. did not subscribe to it, because they thought the establishment not favourable enough: so long as they who did subscribe can support the bank upon the terms of the act of parliament, none will pretend to any share in it; unless the subscribers are pleased to sell. But if other priviledges are given, A. B. and C. as any others of the country may desire the books to be opened, that they be allowed to share in it; and any other set of men who offer the same security, may at the same time be allowed to set up a bank with the same priviledges: so every shire in Scotland will desire one. And if new priviledges are given to this bank, it were a hardship to refuse the same to others, who are able and willing to give the same security, especially when the nation stands in need of more money than this bank would be allowed to give out.

CHAPTER V

That any measures proposed for increasing the silver money or establishing a credit promising a payment of silver money are ineffectual. That silver money has fallen much from the value it had. That land is of greater value. That silver may lose the additional value it received from being used as money.

CHAPTER V

National power and wealth consists in numbers of people, and magazines of home and foreign goods. These depend on trade, and trade depends on money. So to be powerful and wealthy in proportion to other nations, we should have money in proportion with them; for the best laws without money cannot employ the people, improve the product, or advance manufacture and trade.

The measures have been used to preserve and increase money, or such as are now proposed, are attended with difficulties; and tho' the difficulties were removed, are ineffectual, and not capable to furnish money so as to improve the country, or extend trade in any proportion to the improvements and trade of other nations.

Credit that promises a payment of money, cannot well be extended beyond a certain proportion it ought to have with the money. And we have so little money, that any credit could be given upon it, would be inconsiderable.

It remains to be considered, whether any other goods than silver, can be made money with the same safety and convenience.

From what has been said about the nature of money, Chap. I. it is evident, that any other goods which have the qualities necessary in money, may be made money equal to their value, with safety and convenience. There was nothing of humour or fancy in making silver to be money; it was made money, because it was thought best qualified for that use.

I shall endeavour to prove, that another money may be established, with all the qualities necessary in money in a greater degree than silver; with other qualities that silver has not: and preferable for that use, tho' silver were the product of Scotland. And that by this money, the people may be employed, the country improved, manufacture advanced, trade domestick and foreign be carried on, and wealth and power attained.

What I propose, will I hope be found safe, and practicable; advantageous in general to Scotland, and in particular to every Scots-man.

But as I offer to prove, that what I shall propose is more qualified for the use of money than silver: so before I come to the proposal, I shall show some defects in silver money; and that it has not, nor does not answer the design of money.

Money is the measure by which goods are valued, the value by which goods are exchanged, and in which contracts are made payable.

Money is not a pledge, as some call it. It's a value payed, or contracted to be payed, with which 'tis supposed the receiver may, as his occasions require, buy an equal quantity of the same goods he has sold, or other goods equal in value to them: and that money is the most secure value, either to receive, to contract for, or to value goods by; which is least liable to a change in its value.

Silver money is more uncertain in its value than other goods, so less qualified for the use of money.

The power the magistrate has to alter the money in its denomination or fineness, takes away the chief quality for which silver was made money. In countries where the money is often changed in the denomination or fineness, 'tis more uncertain to contract for money, than it was in the state of barter to contract for goods. If a 100 ounces of silver are lent, or contracted for, and a bond given for them denominat pounds, payable in a year: in that time half a crown is raised to a crown, and 50 ounces pays the 100 lent, or contracted for.

Tho' the magistrate did never alter the money in its denomination or fineness, yet it is more uncertain in its value than other goods.

Goods of the same kind and quality differ in value, from any change in their quantity, or in the demand for them: in either of these cases goods are said to be dearer, or cheaper, being more or less valuable, and equal to a greater or lesser quantity of other goods, or of money.

Silver in bullion or money changes its value, from any change in its quantity, or in the demand for it: in either of these cases goods are said to be dearer, or cheaper; but 'tis silver or money is dearer or cheaper, being more or less valuable, and equal to a greater or lesser quantity of goods.

Perishable goods such as corn, &c. increase or decrease in quantity as the demand for them increases or decreases; so their value continues equal or near the same.

More durable goods such as mettals, materials for shipping, &c. increase in quantity beyond the demand for them, so are less valuable.

Silver or money increases in quantity by so much as is imported to Europe, more than is consumed or exported. The demand has encreased, but not in proportion to the quantity.; for, 1st. the same quantity of silver or money won't purchase the same quantity of goods as before. 2dly. 10 per cent was payed for the use of it; now 'tis to be had at 6, in Holland at 3 or 4.

An ounce of silver being worth 5 sh. and 2 pence, and a crown worth 60 pence, unless altered by the prince, makes most people insensible of any change in the value of silver or money: but as one year the boll of barley is sold for 2 crowns, and the year after for 3; this difference comes from a change in the quantity or demand of the barley, or of the money: and that of the money will occasion a difference in the price, as well as that of the barely.

If last year a 100 sheep were sold for a 100 crowns, and the person sold them desires this year to buy the same number of sheep; tho' the quantity of the sheep, and the demand for them be the same as last year: yet if the money is increased in quantity, and the demand for it not increased in proportion, the 100 sheep will be equal in value to more money than the year before, so the money is cheaper. If the quantity of the money, and the demand for it be the same as before; yet if the sheep are lesser in quantity, or the demand for them greater: the 100 sheep will be equal to a greater quantity of money, so the sheep are dearer.

So tho' the magistrate did never alter the money, yet 'tis liable to a change in its value as sliver; from any change in its quantity, or in the demand for it: and the receiver is doubly uncertain whether the money he receives or contracts for, will, when he has occasion, buy him the same goods he has sold, or other goods equal in value to them; because of the difference may happen in the value of the money, or the goods he is to buy.

And this uncertainty is, tho' both money and goods were certain in their quality.

The difference of the prices of most goods, from changes in their quantity, or in the demand for them, would be much prevented, if magazines were kept; but the difference in their prices from the greater or lesser quantity of, or demand for money; cannot be prevented so long as silver is the money.

That money is of much lesser value than it was; will appear by the value goods, land, and money had 200 years ago.

CHAPTER V 61

By the acts of the council of Edinburgh, it appears, that anno 1495, the fiars for wheat was 6 sh. and 8 pennies Scots money the boll.

Anno 1520, claret and white French wines were ordered to be sold in the taverns at 6 pennies Scots the pint, and ale at 20 pennies Scots the gallon.

Anno 1526, the milns belonging to the town were lett for 400 merks Scots, now they give 13000.

The petty customs at Leith then lett for 115 merks.

Anno 1532, the load of malt containing 9 firlots, was ordered to be sold at 32 sh. Scots the load.

Anno 1551, ordered that the best mutton bulk be sold for 12 pennies Scots, the 2d. sort for 10 pennies, and the worst sort for 8 pennies.

Anno 1553, the 9 firlots of malt old measure, with the charity, is ordered to be sold for 36 sh. Scots. The landwart bread to weigh 40 ounces, and the townbread 36 ounces the 4 penny or plack loaf.

Anno 1555, the bakers are ordered for each boll of wheat, to deliver 7 score loafs, at 16 ounces the loaf.

By an act of the 5th parliament of Queen Mary, anno 1551. 'Tis ordained, that wines imported upon the east and north coast, should not be sold dearer than 20 lib. Scots the tun of Bordeaux wine, and 16 lib. the tun of Rochel wine. The pint of Bordeaux wine 10 pennies, and the pint of Rochel wine 8 pennies. And that wine imported upon the west coast, be sold no dearer than 16 lib. Scots the tun of Bordeaux wine, and 12 or 13 lib. the tun of Rochel wine. 8 pennies the pint of Bordeaux wine, and 6 pennies the pint of Rochel wine.

So that what 5 lib. bought 200 years ago, will not be bought now for a 100 lib. Nor were goods in greater plenty, or of less value than now: on the contrair, as these acts were made to regulat the prices of goods, 'tis reasonable to think they were in lesser quantity than now, proportioned to the demand, so of more value. But money having increased in quantity, more than in demand, and having been altered by the prince; is fallen in value: and a 100 lib. now is not worth what 5 lib. was worth before.

Land may be computed to have been improved in 200 years, that what pays now two bolls the acre, payed then but one boll: which may be known from old rentals.

Money gave then 10 per cent interest, and as 384 acres, rented at a boll the acre, victual at 8 sh. and 4 d. the chalder; so the property of these acres was equal to, or worth a 100 lib. for a 100 lib. gave 10 lib. interest, and the 384 acres payed only such a quantity of victual, as was sold for 10 lib. But as land (being preferable to money for many reasons) is valued now at 20 years purchase, tho' money is at 6 per cent: so that land then may have been valued 14 years purchase or 140 lib.

As the quantity of money has increased since that time, much more than the demand for it; and as the same quantity of silver has received a higher denomination, so of consequence money is of lesser value: a lesser interest is given for it: A greater quantity of it is given for the same quantity of goods, and the land is worth more years purchase.

The value of such land now, the acre rented at 2 bolls, victual at 8 lib. 6 sh. and 6 pence, money at 6 per cent, so land at 20 years purchase, would be 8000 lib. By this computation money is only worth the 20th part of goods, and the 57th part of land, it was worth 200 years ago. Part of this difference is from the improvement made on land, and the greater demand for land, the quantity being the same, whereby its value is greater: the rest of the difference is, from the money being more encreased in quantity, than in demand, whereby its value is lesser, and its use lower: as likewise from its being altered in the denomination.

CHAPTER V 63

There was then a greater quantity of silver in the same number of pence than there is now: which appears by several acts of parliament made about that time.

Anno 1475, in the 8 par. of K. James the 3. the ounce of silver was ordered to be sold for 12 sh. Scots, and 12 groats was made of the ounce of silver.

The 3d. of November 1554, by an act of the town-council of Edinburgh, the ounce of silver was ordered to be sold at 18 sh. and 8 pennies Scots; but these acts do not mention the fineness the silver was of. Suppose the same number of pence had twice or 4 times the value of silver in them that they have now: then silver is only fallen to one tenth, or one fifth of the value it had to goods; and to one 28th, or one 14 of the value it had to land. But still money is fallen to one 20th of the value it had to goods, and to one 57th of the value it had to land.

The manner of lending money in France, and I suppose in other Roman Catholick countries; is by way of perpetual interest, redeemable by the debitor, and which the creditor may dispone or assign, but can never demand the principal. And it is usury by law to take any interest for money, if the creditor has power to call for the principal, tho' the term of payment be many years after the money is lent. Suppose the manner of lending in Scotland was the same 200 years ago, and that A. B. having 768 acres of land, rented at a boll of victual the acre, the yearly rent 48 chalder, at 5 lib. Scots the chalder, 20 lib. sterl. C. D. worth a 100 lib. in money, to have lent it to A. B. and interest being at 10 per cent, to have received an annual interest of 10 lib. which he left to his son, and thought he had provided sufficiently for him, 10 lib. being equal to, or worth 24 chalder of victual. But interest being lowered to 6 per cent, money being raised in the denomination, and of less value by its greater quantity: the 6 lib. now paid for the annual interest of that 100 lib. is not worth one chalder of victual. And 384 acres, or the half of A. B.'s land 200 years ago only equal to a 100, or a 140 lib; is now worth 57 times that sum, the rental supposed to be doubled, and its value at 20 years purchase.

In France it has been observed, that about 200 years ago, the same land was in 30 years worth double the money it was worth before. So land worth a 100 lib. anno 1500, was worth 200 lib. anno 1530. 400 lib. anno 1560. And so on, till within these 50 or 60 years it has continued near the same value.

In England, 20 times the quantity of money is given for goods, that was given 200 years ago. In these countries 'tis thought goods have rose; but goods have kept their value, 'tis money has fallen.

Most goods have increased in quantity, equal or near as the demand for them has increased; and are at or near the value they had 200 years ago. Land is more valuable, by improvement producing to a greater value, and the demand increasing, the quantity being the same. Silver and money are of lesser value, being more increased in quantity, than in demand.

Goods will continue equal in quantity as they are now to the demand, or won't differ much: for the increase of most goods depends on the demand. If the quantity of oats be greater than the demand for consumption and magazines, what is over is a drug, so that product will be lessened, and the land imployed to some other use: if by a scarcity the quantity be lesser than the demand, that demand will be supplyed from magazines of former years; or if the magazines are not sufficient to answer the demand, that scarcity cannot well be supposed to last above a year or two.

Land will continue to rise in value, being yet capable of improvement; and as the demand increases, for the quantity will be the same.

Silver will continue to fall in value, as it increases in quantity, the demand not increasing in proportion; for the increase does not depend on the demand. Most people won't allow themselves to think that silver is cheaper or less valuable, tho' it appears plainly, by comparing what quantity of goods such a weight of fine silver bought 200 years ago, and what quantity of the same goods it will buy now. If a piece of wine in France is equal in value to 20 bolls of oats there, that quantity of oats can never be worth more or less wine; so long as the quality, quantity and demand of both continues the same: but any disproportioned change in their quality, quantity or demand, will make the same quantity of the one, be equal to a greater quantity of the other. So if a piece of wine in France, is equal to or worth 40 crowns there; it will always continue so, unless some disproportioned change happen in the quantity, quality, or demand of the wine, or of the money.

The reason is plain, why silver has encreased more in quantity than in demand: the Spaniards bring as great quantities into Europe as they can get wrought out of the mines, for it is still valued tho' not so high. And tho' none of it come into Britain, yet it will be of less value in Britain, as it is in greater quantity in Europe.

It may be objected that the demand for silver is now greater than the quantity. It is answered: tho' the demand is greater than the quantity; yet it has not increased in proportion with the quantity. 200 years ago money or silver was at 10 per cent, now from 6 to 3. If the demand had increased as much as the quantity, money would give 10 p. cent as then, and be equal to the same quantity of victual, or other goods that have kept their value. If A. B. having a 1000 lib. to lend, should offer it at 10 per cent interest, and desired land of 240 chalder of victual rent for his security, as was used to be given 200 years ago: tho' no law regulate the interest of money, A. B. would find no borrowers on these conditions; because silver having increased more in quantity than in demand, and the denomination being altered, money is of less value, and is to be had on easier terms. If the demand had encreased in the same proportion with the quantity, and the money had not been raised, the same interest would be given now as then, and the same quantity of victual to pay the interest; for money keeping its value, 8 sh. and 4 pence would be equal to a chalder of victual, as it was then.

If 2000 lib. were laid out on plate 200 years ago, it is thought the loss on the plate was only the fashion, and the interest; but if the 2000 lib. had been laid out on land, the rent of that land would be more than the value of such plate.

Tho' money or silver is so much fallen from the value it had, yet it's given as a value for one half, or two thirds more than its value as silver, abstract from its use as money.

Suppose silver to be no more used as money in Europe, its quantity would be the same, and the demand for it much lesser; which might lower it 2 thirds or more; for besides that the demand would be less, its uses as plate, &c. are not near so necessary, as that of money.

Goods given as a value, ought for their other uses to be valuable, equal to what they are given for. Silver was bartered as it was valued for its uses as a metal, and was at first given as money, according to the value it had in barter. Silver has acquired an additional value since, that additional use it was applyed to occasioning a greater demand for it; which value people have not been sensible of, the greater quantity making it fall more: but it has kept it from falling so low it would have fallen, if it had not been used as money, and the same quantity had come into Europe.

'Tis uncertain how long silver may keep that additional value: if England set up a money of another kind, silver will not fall to one third, because used in other places as money; but the lesser demand, besides the ordinary fall from the greater quantity coming into Europe, would occasion an extraordinary fall perhaps of 10 per cent: if the new money then in England did not encrease beyond the demand for it, it would keep its value, and be equal to so much more silver at home or abroad than it was coined for; as silver would be of less value, from the ordinary and extraordinary fall.

If England changed their money, other countries may do the same. If Holland alone kept to silver money, the price of silver may be supposed to fall immediately 50 per cent, from the lesser demand for it as money. And 100 lib. in Holland would be worth no more than 50 lib. new money in England, whether sent in specie or remitted by exchange; and as more silver came in to Europe, it would fall yet lower, because of its greater quantity.

It may be objected, that in Scotland the quantity of goods are proportioned to the demand as they have been some years ago; and money scarcer, the demand for it the same or greater. So if goods and money are higher or lower in value, from their greater or lesser quantity in proportion to the demand for them; money should by its great scarcity be more valuable, and equal to a greater quantity of goods. Yet goods differ little in price, from what they were when money was in greater quantity.

To this it's answered, the value of goods or money differs, as the quantity of them or demand for them changes in Europe; not as they change in any particular country. Goods in Scotland are at or near the same value with goods in England, being near the same in quantity in proportion to the demand as there: money in Scotland is not above one 40th part of the money in England, proportioned to the people, land, or product; nor above a 10th part proportioned to the demand. If Scotland was incapable of any commerce with other countries, and in the state it is now, money here would buy 10 times the quantity of goods it does in England, or more: but as Scotland has commerce with other countries, tho' money were much scarcer than now, or in much greater quantity than in England; if there were but 10000 lib. in Scotland, or a million, the value of goods would not differ above 30 per cent, from what they were abroad, because for that difference goods may be exported, or imported, prohibitions may raise the difference higher.

Britannia Languens, and others on trade and money, are of opinion that goods in any country fall in value, as money in that particular country grows scarcer. That, if there was no more than 500 lib. in England, the yearly rent of England would not exceed 500 lib. and an ox would be sold for a penny. Which opinion is wrong, for as the ox might be exported to Holland, it would give a price in England equal or near to that it would give in Holland: if money were supposed to be equally scarce in Holland, and other places as in England, the ox might give no more than a penny, but that penny would have a value then equal to 5 lib. now; because it would purchase the same quantity of goods in England or other places, that 5 lib. does now.

The same answer may be given to these who think an addition to the money of any particular country would undervalue it so, that the same quantity of goods would cost double the money as before.

If the money and credit current in England be 15 millions, Scotland reckoned as 1 to 10, the money in Scotland encreased to a million and a half, the demand in proportion to the demand in England; that addition to the money of Scotland, would not make money of less value here, than it is now in England. Goods in Scotland would sell as they sell in England, the product of the country would perhaps be 10 or 20 per cent dearer, to bring it equal to what it sells in England; but all sorts of manufacture would be cheaper, because in greater quantity: and all goods imported would be cheaper, money being easier borrowed, merchants would deal for a greater value, and men of estates would be capacitate to trade, and able to sell at less profit. Nor would land rise higher than in England, the buyer having in his choice to buy elsewhere; the better security of a register may be supposed to add a year's purchase or two to the value.

If the money of any particular country should encrease beyond the proportion that country bears to Europe; it would undervalue money there, or, according to the way of speaking, it would raise goods: but as money would be undervalued every where the same, or near to what it were there; it would be of great advantage to that country, tho' thereby money were less valuable: for that country would have the whole benefit of the greater quantity, and only bear a share of the lesser value, according to the proportion its money had to the money of Europe. When the Spaniards bring money or bullion into Europe, they lessen its value, but gain by bringing it; because they have the whole benefit of the greater quantity, and only bear a share of the lesser value.

What has been said, proves, 1st. That silver money is an uncertain value; because lyable to be altered in the fineness or denomination by the prince. A crown has no more silver in it than half a crown or 15 pence had 150 or 200 years ago.

2dly. That as silver has fallen from the value it had, the same quantity not being worth the 5th or 10th part of what it was worth then. A moneyed man then worth a 1000 lib. was richer at that time than a landed man of 240 chalder of victual rent: but a man of such a money estate, would not now be worth one 50th part of such a land estate.

3dly. That tho' fallen so much, yet it is given as money or sold as bullion, for much more than its value as a metal; to which it will be reduced, so soon as another money is set up.

Considering the present state of Europe, France and Spain being masters of the mines, the other nations seem to be under a necessity of setting up another money. The only reason can be given why it has not yet been done, is, that the nature of money has not been rightly understood: or they would not have continued buying silver from Spain above its value as a metal, when they had a more valuable money of their own; and every way more fitted for that use.

The receiver of silver can have no great hopes that the value of it will be greater; for 'tis not to be supposed it will be apply'd to any other uses, than it is now apply'd to, whereby the demand for it may be encreas'd: or that the quantity exported and consum'd, will be greater than the quantity imported.

Tho' it be scarce in any particular country, yet the money'd men will have no great benefit by such scarcity, as has been shown: for unless the scarcity is the same in all places with which that country trades, money will not be valued much higher there than in other countries.

If it is alleged the mines in the West Indies may fail. 'Tis the interest of the Spaniards to give out that their mines begin to fail, to keep up the price of silver; but if that were true, France ought not to have engaged her self in a war, when by the partition treaty she could have got any other parts of that monarchy that are valuable. Allowing the mines do fail, we ought the rather to provide ourselves with another money.

CHAPTER VI

The proposal given in to Parliament by Dr. H. C. examined.

CHAPTER VI

I did not intend to have said anything about the Dr's proposal, that affair having been referr'd to a committee, who are to make their report. But several people who are of opinion that the Dr's proposal is not practicable, being against what I am to propose, because they think 'tis the same with his in some other dress: I thought it needful to give a short account of the Dr's proposal, and in what I differ from him.

His proposal is to give out notes upon land, to be cancell'd by yearly payments of about 2 and a quater per cent, for 45 years. And that these notes be current as silver money, to the value they are coin'd for.

If notes given out after that manner, were equal in value to silver money; then every landed man in Scotland would desire a share of this great and certain advantage: and I don't see how it is practicable to give every landed man a share.

Supposing it practicable, 45 years purchase in these notes, will not be of so much value, as 20 years purchase of silver money.

No anticipation is equal to what already is. A years rent now is worth 15 years rent 50 years hence, because that money let out at interest, by that time will produce so much. And tho' the parliament would force these notes, yet they would not have currency, any more than if the government coin'd pieces of gold equal in weight and fineness, with a guinea, and ordered them to pass for 5 lib.

These bills are propos'd to be repay'd and cancell'd in a term of years, without paying any interest, but only so much as would defray the charges of the office, which would not be above one half per cent.

There would then be many lenders, but few if any borrowers, except from the land bank: for as 'tis the landed man borrows of the money'd man, he would satisfie his creditor, and have bills to lend. The money'd man would likewise have of these bills to lend, but there would be no borrowers; or if any desired to borrow, they would have these bills at a very low use. Suppose at 2 per cent, then these bills would be considerably less valuable than silver.

Anything that is propos'd to have a currency as money, and is given for a lesser interest than silver money, will be of less value.

It is not to be supposed any person will lend silver money at 2 per cent when they can have 6 per cent in England. So a 100 lib. silver money, will yield as much as 300 lib. of these bills would: and 100 lib. in silver, will be equal to 300 lib. in bills. The 6 lib. the 100 lib. of silver yields, being silver, and the 6 lib. the 300 of bills yields, being payed in these bills: and 1 lib. silver, being worth 3 lib. in bills; so the 6 lib. interest of the 100 lib. in silver, would be equal to 18 lib. or the interest of 900 lib. in bills.

And tho' they were given out to be repay'd in 20 years, at 5 per cent for that time; or in 10 years, at 10 per cent: they would not be equally valuable with silver. The difference would not be so great, as when given out for 45 years.

The advantage the nation would have by the Dr's proposal is; that tho' these notes sell under the value of silver money, and

500 lib. in notes were only equal to a 100 lib. in silver; yet the nation would have the same advantage by that 500 lib. in notes, as if an addition of a 100 lib. had been made to the silver money.

So far as these bills sell under the value of the silver money, so far would exchange with other countries be rais'd. And if goods did not keep their price, (i.e.) if they did not sell for a greater quantity of these bills, equal to the difference betwixt them and silver: goods exported would be undervalued, and goods imported would be overvalued, as has been explain'd on page 24[1] about exchange.

The landed-man would have no advantage by this proposal, unless he owed debt: for tho' he received 50 lib. of these bills, for the same quantity of victual he was in use to receive, 10 lib. silver money; yet that 50 lib. would only be equal in value to 10 lib. of silver, and purchase only the same quantity of home or foreign goods.

The landed-man who had his rent pay'd him in money, would be a great loser. For by as much as these bills were under the value of silver, he would receive so much less than before.

The landed-man who owed debt, would pay his debt with a less value than was contracted for: but the creditor would lose what the debtor gain'd.

Dr. C. seems to be offended at my meddling in this affair, having, as he says, borrow'd what I know of this subject from him. Two persons may project the same thing, but so far as I can judge, what I am to propose is different from his, and what I had form'd a scheme of several years before I had seen any of his papers: which I can prove, if that were necessary, by persons of worth I then show'd it to. I have not, to my knowledge, borrowed any thing from Dr. C. Land indeed is the value upon which he founds his proposal, and 'tis upon land that I found

---

1. Pages 43 and 44 of the 1750 edition.

mine: if for that reason I have incroached upon his proposal, the bank of Scotland may be said to have done the same: there were banks in Europe long before the Dr's proposal, and books have been writ on the subject before and since. The foundation I go upon has been known so long as money has been lent on land, and so long as an heretable bond has been equal to a quantity of land. Whether the structure he or I have built upon that foundation be most safe, advantageous and practicable, the parliament can best judge.

Dr. C's proposal is by anticipation, to make land worth 50 or 100 years purchase; and maintains that a 100 lib. to be payed yearly for 10, 50, or a 100 years, is a valuable pledge for a 1000, 5000, or 10000 lib. a of bills: and that these bills will be equal to silver money. If he can satisfie the nation that his proposal is practicable, he does a very great service, and gives a certain advantage to the landed-man, without wronging the money'd-man. I have shown the reasons why I think the proposal is not practicable; and that notwithstanding any act of parliament made to force these bills, they would fall much under the value of silver. but allowing they were at first equal to silver, it is next to impossible that two different species of money, shall continue equal in value to one another.

Every thing receives a value from its use, and the value is rated, according to its quality, quantity and demand. Tho' goods of different kinds are equal in value now, yet they will change their value, from any unequal change in their quality, quantity, or demand.

And as he leaves it to choice of the debtor, to pay in silver-money or bills, he confines the value of the bills, to the value of the silver-money, but cannot confine the value of the silver-money to the value of the bills: so that these bills must fall in value as silver-money falls, and may fall lower: silver may rise above the value of these bills, but these bills cannot rise above the value of silver.

What I shall propose, is to make money of land equal to its value; and that money to be equal in value to silver-money; and not lyable to fall in value as silver money falls.

Any goods that have the qualities necessary in money, may be made money equal to their value. 5 ounces of gold is equal in value to 20 lib. and may be made money to that value. An acre of land rented at 2 bolls of victual, the victual at 8 lib. and land at 20 years purchase, is equal to 20 lib. and may be made money equal to that value, for it, has all the qualities necessary in money. But that acre of land cannot be coin'd to the value of 50 lib. no more than the 5 ounces of gold. And tho' the 5 ounces of gold, the 20 lib. silver-money and the acre of land, be now equal in value; yet they cannot well continue so: for as I have shown already, any disproportion'd change in the quality, quantity, or in the demand of either of them, will make the same quantity of the one, equal to a greater or lesser quantity of the others. Land is what in all appearance will keep its value best, it may rise in value, but cannot well fall: gold or silver are lyable to many accidents, whereby their value may lessen; but cannot well rise in value.

CHAPTER VII

The proposal with reasons for it.

CHAPTER VII

To supply the nation with money, it is humbly propos'd, that 40 commissioners be appointed by parliament, answerable to parliament for their administration, and the administration of the officers under them: the nomination of these officers being left to the commissioners.

That the commissioners have power to coin notes: which notes to be received in payments, where offer'd.

That a committee of parliament be appointed to inspect the management, and that none of the commissioners be members.

That the commission and committee meet twice a year at Whitsunday and Martinmass; their meetings, to begin 10 days before, and to continue 10 days after each term.

There are three ways humbly offer'd to the parliament, for giving out these notes: they in their wisdom may determine which will be most safe.

1. To authorize the commission to lend notes on land security, the debt not exceeding one half, or two thirds of the value: and at the ordinary interest.

2. To give out the full price of land, as it is valued, 20 years purchase more or less, according to what it would have given in silver-money, the commission entering into possession of such

lands, by wadset granted to the commission or assigneys; and redeemable betwixt and the expiring of a term of years.

3. To give the full price of land, upon sale made of such lands, and disponed to the commission or assigneys irredeemably.

That any person shall have such bonds, wadsets or estates assigned or dispon'd to them, upon paying in the value to the commission.

That the Commission don't receive other money than these notes.

That no person who has contracted for these notes, shall be obliged to receive silver or metal money.

That the commission have not power to coin more than 50000 lib. at a time, and that no more be coin'd so long as there is 25000 lib. remaining in the office.

That for a year and a half the commission be limited to a certain sum, after that time to have power to coin what sums are demanded: unless restricted by ensuing parliaments.

That these who desire to have money from the commission, give in a note to the lawyers for the commission, a month before the term, of what sums they want, with the rights of the lands they offer in pledge: and that these who have notes to pay in to the commission, give warning 10 days before the term.

That the state of the commission, the sum of notes coin'd, the debt and credit, with the highest number of the different notes, be publish'd every term.

That any person who shall discover 2 notes of the same number, or of a higher number than these publish'd, shall have a 100 lib. reward.

That the under-officers be intrusted with the sum of 20000 lib. to change notes with; and that they attend the whole year.

That any member of parliament may inspect the state of

the commission.

That no notes be coined, money lent, or rights assigned by the commission, but at the terms of Whitsunday and Martinmass: and in presence of at least 20 commissioners, and one third of the committee.

That the revenue of the commission, over what pays the charges, and what part the parliament thinks needful to make good any losses may happen to the commission, be applyed by way of drawback, for encouraging the export, and manufacture of the nation.

That paper-money does not rise more than 10 per cent above silver-money; so that he who contracts to pay in paper, may know what he is to pay in case he cannot get paper money.

The parliament may enter into a resolve, that the next sessions of this or the next ensuing parliament, the state of the commission be taken into consideration, preferable to all other business: and if found hurtful to the country, the parliament may discharge any more notes to be given out, and order what notes are then out to be called in.

That after 3 months from the date of the act, Scots and foreign money be reduced to the English standard. The English crown to 60 pence, and the other money in proportion to its value of silver. The 40 pence to 38 pence, the new mark to 13 pence and one third; the old mark to its weight, the ducatdowns to 68 pence, dollars to their weight. Guineas not to pass 22 sh.

That after 4 months no Scots money (except what shall be coined after the Act), nor any foreign money except the English money, be received in any payments, or be sold as bullion but at the mint.

That for what old money or bullion is brought to the mint, the mint return to the full value in new money of 12 pence, 6 pence, and 3 pence pieces; of 11 deniers fine, the 12 pence of three drops 3 grains weight, the other pieces to weigh in proportion: the expence of coinage to be payed out of the funds appropriated to that use.

That for 3 months after the act, the new money pass for 13 pence, 6 pence half-penny, and 3 pence and one quarter.

That after 3 months, bullion and wrought plate be of 11 deniers fine, and 5 sh. and 2 d. the ounce of silver, gold not to pass 4 lib.

The paper-money proposed will be equal in value to silver, for it will have a value of land pledg'd equal to the same sum of silver-money that it is given out for. If any losses should happen, one 4th of the revenue of the commission, will in all appearance be more than sufficient to make them good.

This paper-money will not fall in value as silver-money has fallen, or may fall: goods or money fall in value, if the increase in quantity, or if the demand lessens. But the commission giving out what sums are demanded, and taking back what sums are offered to be returned; this paper-money will be keep its value, and there will always be as much money as there is occasion, or employment for, and no more.

If a contract for paper-money could be satisfied by paying the same quantity of silver money, then that paper-money could not rise above the value of silver, and would fall with it. But as the paper money is a different species from silver, so it will not be lyable to any of the changes silver money is lyable to.

Tho' the parliament could give silver money to the people, in as great quantity as there were occasion: the parliament could not justly know what sum would serve the country, for the demand changes. If the quantity of money is less than the demand, the landed man is wronged: for a 100 lib. then being more valuable, will buy a greater quantity of the landed mans goods. If the quantity of money is greater than the demand, the money'd-man is wronged, for a 100 lib. then is not so valuable, so will not buy the same quantity of goods a 100 lib. bought before.

If the commission do not give out money when it is demanded, where good security is offer'd; 'tis a hardship on the person who is refused, and a loss to the country: for few if any borrow money to keep by them; and if employed it brings a profit to the nation, tho' the employer loses.

If the commission did not take back what sums were offer'd to be returned, it were a hardship on the money'd man, who has a sum payed him, and does not know how to employ it; and the quantity being greater than the demand for it, would fall in value.

After the method propos'd, the quantity being always equal to the demand for it, it will keep its value, and buy the same quantity of goods 50 years hence, as now: unless the goods alter in their value, from any change in their quantity, or in the demand for them.

Suppose this commission had been established 200 years ago, land then at 14 years purchase, money at 10 per cent, victual at 8 shil. and 4 pence the chalder, and paper money to have been given out upon land; 8 shil. and 4 pence of that paper money, would now have been equal to a chalder of victual, and to 8 lib. 6 sh. and 4 pence silver-money: because silver-money having increas'd in quantity, more than the demand; and having been alter'd in the denomination, has fallen to one 20th of the value it had then. Nor would the landed man have receiv'd less for his victual, than now; for that paper-money would have bought him 20 times the quantity of goods, silver-money will buy.

Land has a more certain value than other goods, for it does not increase in quantity, all other goods may. The uses of goods may be discharged, or by custom be taken from them, and given to other goods: the use of bread may be taken from oats, and wholly given to wheat: the use of money may be taken from silver, and given to land: the use of plate, and the other uses of silver as a metal, may be taken from silver, and given to some other metal, or some mixture that may be more fitted for these uses. In any of these cases, these goods lose a part of their value, proportion'd to the uses are taken from them: but land cannot lose any of its uses. For, as every thing is produced by land, so the land must keep its value, because it can be turn'd to produce the goods that are in use. If wheat is more us'd and oats less, as the land can produce both, it will be turn'd to produce what is most used, because most valuable.

This money will not receive any additional value from being used as money, so the receiver will be certain he can be no loser, tho' after a term of years the use of money is taken from it. The land will receive an additional value, from being used as the pledge upon which the money is issued; and that additional value would be greater than what silver received: because, tho' land be used as the pledge to issue out money upon, yet none of its other uses would be taken from it: silver cannot be us'd as money and plate at the same time. But as land is in greater quantity than there will be occasion for to give out money upon; so the additional value it receives, will not be near so great as that silver-money has receiv'd.

Suppose the additional value land received were one 4th, land now at 20 years purchase, would then be at 25 years purchase. If the parliament call'd in the paper money, he who had paper money could be no loser by it, tho' the land lost the additional value; for no more of it is given out than the value of the land abstract from its use as money. Whereas if silver was no more used as money, he who had silver, would lose a half, or 2 thirds; silver falling then to its value as a metal.

So that this paper money propos'd, having a better value than silver; and receiving no addition to its value, from being used as money; and not being lyable to any change in its value, the quantity and demand encreasing and decreasing together: it is so far more qualified to be the measure by which goods are valued, the value by which goods are exchanged, and in which contracts are made payable.

The other qualities necessary in money, are:

1. Easy of delivery.
2. Of the same value in one place to what it is in another.
3. To be kept without loss or expence.
4. To be divided without loss.
5. To be capable of a stamp.

Paper money has each of the above qualities in a greater degree than silver:

1. It is easier of delivery: 500 lib. in paper may be payed in less time, than 5 lib. in silver.

2. It is nearer the value in one place to what it is in another, being of easier carriage.

3. It can be easier kept; taking up less room. And without loss; because it may be exchanged at the office. The consumption of paper is not of so much value as the consumption of sliver: the consumption of the paper is a loss to the office, the consumption of silver is a loss to the owner.

4. It can be divided without loss: because it may be changed for lesser notes at the office.

5. It is capable of a stamp, and less liable to be counterfeit.

The practice of more trading nations confirms, that paper is more qualified for the use of money, than silver; providing it hath a value. In Holland, silver is pledg'd, and paper is used as money. That land pledg'd is a better value than silver pledg'd, is evident from what has been said. In England, before the bank was set up, goldsmiths notes were received in payments preferable to gold or silver: which shows that paper money had all the qualities necessary in money, so much more than gold or silver, as to equal the danger of a gold-smith's breaking, of which there were many examples. Mr. Lock, pag. 7 on interest of money, says, that one goldsmith's credit (being usually a note under one of his servants hands) went for above eleven hundred thousand pounds at a time.

The notes of the bank in Scotland went, tho' there was no money in the bank, and tho' their acceptance was voluntary. The security for the paper propos'd will be as good, the administration may be more safe and satisfactory than that bank, or any other private bank; because it is more public, and the commission has not any share of the profits. Besides, it will not be liable to the hazard banks are liable to, from the sale of shares.

And it seems strange that the administration of such a commission should be doubted, when the parliament has the nomination of the managers; when the managers are to be accountable to the parliament; when the trust is to be so small, for more notes cannot be coin'd so long as 25000 lib. is in the office; a committee of parliament is to be appointed to inspect the management, the books are to be open to the inspection of any member of parliament, and the state of the commission is to be published in print.

Since the notes of the bank went upon a voluntary acceptance, tho' there was no money in bank; 'tis reasonable to think the paper money propos'd will at least have the same currency: being current by law does not make it less valuable. He who took bank notes, could not be sure the bank would be in a condition to give money for them; and the person he was to pay money to, might refuse them: so he was more uncertain, than if they had been current by law.

The silver money being to fall betwixt 8 and 9 per cent in 3 months, it is not to be suppos'd that silver will be prefer'd to paper money; since the notes of the bank, which is paper upon the same fund, went at the ordinary interest: and tho' the receiver was not certain of the money at the time it was promised, or that the person he was owing to would receive it.

It may be objected, that paper went because silver could be got for it when demanded, or at a certain time.

That was very reasonable, but would not be so in this case: the security pledg'd for that paper money, was silver. The security pledg'd for this paper money is land. This money has no relation to gold or silver, more than to other goods. And it were more extravagant to say, I won't take a 100 lib. of such paper money for the goods I sell, because I am not sure if 6 months hence it will buy me such a quantity of silver; for silver may grow dearer: as it would be to say now, I won't take a 100 lib. in silver for the goods I sell; because I am not sure if 6 months hence, it will buy me such a quantity of wine, for wine may grow dearer.

4 crowns won't buy a guinea, tho' they were coin'd for the same value; nor won't buy the 10th part of goods 4 crowns bought 200 years ago, yet silver is received as a value, and contracted for, tho' its value lessens every year, and tho' 'tis not perhaps worth above a third of what 'tis given or contracted for, abstract from the use of money. This paper propos'd will not only keep its value; the encrease of the quantity depending on the demand, and the quantity decreasing as the demand decreases: but likewise the land pledg'd is as valuable as the paper given out, abstract from its use as money, and encreases in value.

The objection may be made against silver money, and with good reason; for it falls faster in its value than other goods, and may soon be reduced to its value as a metal.

The paper money propos'd is equal to itself; but to continue equal to such a quantity of any other goods, is to have a quality that no goods can have: for that depends on the changes in these other goods. It has a better and more certain value than silver money, and all the other qualities necessary in money in a much greater degree, with other qualities that silver has not, and is more capable of being made money than anything yet known. Land is what is most valuable, and what encreases in value more than other goods; so the paper money issued from it will, in all appearance, not only keep equal to other goods, but rise above them.

Because of the extraordinary scarcity of silver in Scotland, and the inclination people have to it, from its having been long used as money; it may be necessary to restrict its price to 5 sh. and 2 pence the ounce: but it will soon fall from that value of paper, if it come in greater quantity into Europe, than is exported or consum'd.

Suppose an island belonging to one man, the number of tenents a 100, each tenent 10 in a family, in all a 1000; by these the island is labour'd, part to the product of corns, the rest for pasturage: besides the tenents and their families, there are 300 poor or idle, who live by charity. There is no money, but rents are paid in kind, and if one tenent has more of one product, and less of another than his family has occasion for, he barters with his neighbour.

The people of this island know nothing of manufacture; the island being plentiful, furnishes enough for their consumption, and an overplus which they exchange on the continent for cloaths, and what other goods they want: but as that overplus is only sufficient to make a return of such a quantity of goods as they consume yearly, so they have no magazines of their own or foreign goods to serve them in bad years, nor no magazines of arms, ammunition, &c. for their defence.

'Tis proposed to the proprietor, that if a money were establish'd to pay the wages of labour, the 300 poor might be imployed in manufacturing such goods as before were exported in product; and as the 1000 that labour the ground were idle one half of their time, they might be imployed so as their additional labour would be equal to that of 500 more, which would lessen their import by providing them with a part of such goods as before they brought from the continent, and raise their export to 3 or 4 times the value it had: the return of which would furnish them with greater quantities of foreign goods than they wanted for consumption, which might be laid up in magazines.

The money propos'd is after this manner. The proprietor to coin pieces of paper figured number 1, number 2, and so on; number 4 to be equal to a certain measure of corn. The poor and other labourers would be satisfied to take number 4 for the wages of a day's labour, providing it be so contriv'd that number 4 purchase them the measure of corn; for as that corn can be barter'd with other goods, so number 4 would purchase an equal value of any other goods.

To make number 4 equal to that measure of corn, the proprietor calls his tenents together; tells them for the future, he will have his rent payed in paper so renews their leases, and where a 100 measures of corn was payed, they oblige themselves to pay him number 400. The other kinds the proprietor was payed in are valued, according to the value they had in barter with corn; and leases made for paper.

The proprietor coins paper to the value of a year's rent, imploys such as are willing to work, and gives them paper-money as the price of their labour. The tenent gives corn or any other goods he has to the labourers for paper-money, and the proprietor receives it for his rent. But as the consumption of the labouring man may be suppos'd to be only equal to number 2; so the tenents cannot get the whole sum issued by the proprietor, and consequently not enough to pay their rent. If this were not remeeded, the labouring men being masters of the remaining part of the paper, and having no occasion for more goods from the tenents, might raise the value of the paper. To prevent this, the proprietor coins a greater quantity, which brings a part of the poor and idle of the continent to the island, and occasions a greater consumption, whereby the tenants are able to pay their rent in paper as contracted for. The addition to the people is an advantage to the island; for it adds to the power of the island, and their labour is worth double what they consume.

This money tho' it has no value but what the proprietor gives it, by receiving it in payments of his rent; yet it will be esteem'd equal to the product payed before.

If the proprietor would give it a value in land, computing after this manner: an acre of land pays number 100, at 20 years purchase worth number 2000. And disposes the property of land for paper at that value; who would not be satisfied to receive or contract for that money, since it not only bought the product, but the property of land at a reasonable price?

Money is not the value for which goods are exchanged, but the value by which they are exchanged: the use of money is to buy goods, and silver, while money, is of no other use.

Tho' silver were our product, yet it is not so proper to be made money as land. Land is what produces everything, silver is only the product. Land does not increase or decrease in quantity, silver or any other product may. So land is more certain in its value than silver, or any other goods.

Land is capable of improvement, and the demand for it may be greater; so it may be more valuable. Silver cannot be suppos'd to be apply'd to any other uses, than to which it is now apply'd to; or that the demand will encrease more than the quantity.

Land cannot lose any of its uses, so will not be less valuable; sliver may lose the use of money it is now apply'd to, so be reduc'd to its value as a metal.

It may likewise lose a part of its uses as a metal, these uses being supply'd by other goods: so loses a part of its value as a metal. But nothing can supply the uses of land.

Land may be convey'd by paper, and thereby has the other qualities necessary in money, in a greater degree than silver.

Land has other qualities fitting it for the use of money that silver has not.

Land apply'd to the use of money, does not lose any of the other uses it is apply'd to: silver cannot serve the use of money, and any of its other uses as a metal.

Trade and money depend mutually on one another; when trade decays, money lessens; and when money lessens, trade decays. Power and wealth consist in numbers of people, and magazines of home and foreign goods; these depend on trade, and trade on money. So while trade and money may be effected directly and consequentially, that which is hurtful to either, must be so to both, power and wealth will be precarious.

If a money is establish'd that has no intrinsick value, and its extrinsick value to be such, as it will not be exported; nor will not be less than the demand for it within the country: wealth and power will be attained, and be less precarious. Money not being liable to be lessen'd directly, nor consequentially; and trade not liable to decay consequentially. So the power and wealth of that country will only be precarious, from what may be directly hurtful to trade.

The paper money propos'd being always equal in quantity to the demand, the people will be employ'd, the country improv'd, manufacture advanc'd, trade domestick and foreign will be carried on, and wealth and power attained. And not being liable to be exported, the people will not be set idle, &c. and wealth and power will be less precarious.

From whence it is evident, that land is more qualified for the use of money than silver; and preferable for that use tho' silver were the product of Scotland: being more certain in its value, and having the qualities necessary in money, in a greater degree: with other qualities that silver has not; so more capable of being the general measure by which goods are valued, the value by which goods are exchanged, and in which contracts are taken.

If 2000 lib. of paper money, is equal to the property of land worth 2000 lib. in silver; then that 2000 lib. of paper money, is equal to 2000 lib. of silver.

What buys land, will buy every thing the land produces; and what buys the product of land, will buy all other goods whether home or foreign. If wine is brought from France, the merchant designs to lay out his money on goods, at interest, or on land: the commission does not receive silver money, so he cannot have a bond from the commission, unless he give the value in paper; and many of the landed men won't take silver for their goods or lands, having occasion for paper to pay the commission. So the merchant will choose to sell his wines for paper money, because it will purchase him goods, bonds or lands where silver money will, being equally valuable: and in cases where silver money will not.

And this is supposing silver were equally qualified for the use of money, as land is. But as silver is an uncertain value, and is given for much more than its value as a metal; and has not all the qualities necessary in money, nor in so great a degree as paper money: so paper money will for these other reasons be preferr'd to silver.

Some object that a paper money tho' upon a good fund, and current in the country; yet will not be valued abroad, equal to what it were in Scotland.

The goods of Scotland will always be valued abroad, equal to goods of the same kind and goodness; and that money tho' of paper, which buys goods in Scotland, will buy goods or money in other places. If a 1000 lib. in serges, linen cloth, &c.

be worth abroad all charges payed 1300 lib. the merchant who exports such goods, will give a bill for that money at the par, having 1300 lib. for what cost him a 1000.

When a nation establishes a money, if the money they set up, have a value equal to what it is made money for, and all the other qualities necessary in money; they ought to have no regard what value it will have in other countries. On the contrair, as every country endeavours by laws to preserve their money, if that people can contrive a money that will not be valued abroad; they will do what other countries have by laws endeavour'd in vain.

No nation keeps to silver because it is used in other countries, it is because they can find nothing so safe and convenient. Trade betwixt nations is carried on by exchange of goods, and if one merchant sends out goods of a less value, than he brings home; he has money furnish'd him abroad by another who brings home for a less value than he sent out: if there is no money due abroad, then the merchant who designed to import for a greater value than he exported, is restricted; and can only import equal to his export, which is all the many laws to regulate trade have been endeavouring.

It is objected that we are under a necessity of having goods from countries who will take none of ours. France does not allow money to be exported, nor any ship to import goods, unless French goods are exported from the same port; to the value of the goods which were imported. By our law we are forbid to export money. But as I don't think the example of nations a good answer, I shall endeavour to give a better. Suppose our money is not valued abroad, and we have occasion for goods from Denmark, who takes none of ours. These goods being necessary here, will be valued higher than other goods that are not so necessary; and the value of Scots goods sold in other countries, will be carried to Denmark, in such goods as will sell there, or in foreign money, and these necessary goods be brought home: because the trader makes a greater profit by them, than by such goods as could have been imported from that country, where the goods exported were sold.

But as this addition to the money will employ the people who are now idle, and these now employ'd to more advantage: so the product will be encreas'd, and manufacture advanc'd. If the consumption of the nation continues as now, the export will be greater, and a ballance due to us: and as the exchange depends on the ballance, so paper money here, will be equal to a greater quantity of silver money abroad.

Suppose the yearly value of Scotland a million and a half, the yearly value of England 40 millions; the value of Scotland, is only about one 28th part of the value of England. Yet the quantity and quality of the lands, and the numbers of people considered; Scotland will be at least as 1 to 6. And if there was money to employ the people, we would be as 1 to 6; for we have advantages peculiar to us, that do more than equal the Plantation and East India trades.

England is not improv'd so far as it might be, by a greater quantity of money. We may have money equal to the demand, by applying our land to that use. So our country may be improv'd above the proportion of one to 6. But if the propos'd addition to our money, improved the country only so as to bear a proportion with England of one to 13, our yearly value would be 3 millions: and our consumption not being half what the same number of people consume in England; if the consumption continued as now, the ballance due to Scotland would be greater, than the ballance due to England.

This addition to our yearly value may be thought by some people, a supposition that's extravagant, but I desire these people will consider what consequences the plenty of money has had in other places. As the money of England has increas'd, the yearly value has increas'd; and as the money has decreas'd, the yearly value has decreas'd.

I don't doubt but the paper-money propos'd being given out equal to the demand, would bring the yearly value of Scotland to 3 millions, tho' the fishing and other branches of foreign trade (which might be improv'd to great advantage) were neglected. But suppose the yearly value increas'd only half a million, of which a 4th spent in a greater consumption of the product and manufacture of the country, a 4th in the greater consumption of foreign goods and expence abroad, a 4th laid up in magazines of foreign goods, a 4th would still be due of ballance and brought home in silver.

If the consumption and expence increas'd equal to, or beyond the improvement; as the paper-money could not be exported, so the people would not be set idle nor the manufacture decay: that money being like an estate intail'd. We might continue to consume equal to the yearly value, but could not lessen the yearly value, nor be poorer if we would.

If a greater value of goods was imported than was exported, and credit given for the ballance; foreigners to pay themselves, would send a lesser value of goods the year after. But such restrictions may be put on the consumption of our own and foreign goods, as may make a ballance due.

The revenue of the commission will be a great help toward the advancing our trade in its infancy: what encourages the export of goods, encourages the manufacture of them; and that money given as a draw-back, will not only encourage the export and manufacture; but likewise regain the reputation our goods have lost, and give them a better reputation than the goods of other nations.

The draw-back ought not to be given to all goods, but to such as do not yield a reasonable profit abroad, and upon condition they are sound sufficient.

The seal of the office of draw-back ought to be apply'd to these goods that receive the draw-back; and these intrusted with the draw-back, should give security to pay the price of such goods, with all charges, if found insufficient.

When manufacture and trade prospers, the landed man's rent is well payed, and increases: when they decay, his rent is ill payed, and decreases. A draw-back is so effectual a way to encourage and promote manufacture and trade; that it were the landed men's interest to tax themselves, rather than a draw-back should not be given, where it is necessary.

A draw-back is more necessary here than in other countries, for we do not manufacture so well as other nations: we are not able to sell for the same profit, our stocks being much smaller; and the goods of other nations will be preferr'd to ours, because our goods are suspected.

Some object that this proposal is new, and has not been practis'd in any nation.

The example of another nation ought not to determine us, to follow the same measures, without examining whether that nation was the better or the worse by such measures; and whether our circumstances and theirs don't differ so, as to make that hurtful or ineffectual to us, which was of advantage to them. On the other hand, it is no argument against any thing propos'd for the general good, to say it is new, and what has not been practis'd.

When anything propos'd has been already practis'd by other nations, 'tis a presumption in favours of such a proposal; and it's a presumption against it, if it has been refused: but a wise nation ought not to be determined by example, to follow or refuse without examining.

This proposal has not been refus'd. The essential part is now practis'd in France, for paper is current by law: and tho' after a manner that in all appearance ought to have hindered its currency, yet I'm inform'd foreign bills are bought with paper money, the same as with silver or gold.

The example of nations in relation to money would be a very uncertain rule. For as has been said page 37[1], opposite measures have been us'd in some countries to what have been used in others, and contrary measures have been used in the same countries to what was used immediately before, not because of any difference in their circumstances, but from the opinion, that since the method used had not the effect design'd, a contrary would; and there are good reasons to think that the nature of money is not yet rightly understood.

Any other objections that I have yet heard against this proposal, are such as may be fully answered, and so far as I can see into it, with all the application I have been capable of, I cannot find any objection but what may be fully answer'd; nor any difficulty in the execution, but what may be removed: if there is any fallacy in the positions I lay down, or any wrong consequences drawn from these positions, I have not been able to discover them.

---

1. Page 70 of the 1750 edition.

CHAPTER VIII

The low condition this country is reduced to, notwithstanding its natural advantages.

CHAPTER VIII

The natural advantages the Dutch have for trade, are, their situation at the mouths of the rivers of Germany, and being near the bulky trade.

Their natural disadvantages are, smallness of territory, barrenness of soil, producing little but what's forc'd; want of mines; long winters; un-wholsome air; marishy, so obliged to great expence for foundation to their buildings, in making and keeping up the high-ways, and in draining the country yearly; a dangerous coast; difficult entry to their rivers; the sea to defend against on one side, and powerful neighbours on the other; and heavy taxes, the consequence of these other disadvantages.

Yet they have so improv'd their few advantages, that they are become a rich and powerful people. What has contributed to their riches and power, was the early protection and favour the government gave to trade; the liberty which was given to people of different religions; the freedom of trade allowed to strangers; the example of their rulers in oeconomy; but chiefly the neglect of trade in other countries, particularly in Spain, who forced the people and trade of Flanders to Holland.

Scotland has by nature many advantages for trade; a large territory; of easie defence; plenty of people; a wholsome air; mines; a proper situation for the eastern and western trades;

near the bulky trade; a safe coast; rivers of easie entry; the seas and rivers stockt with fish.

But numbers of people, the greatest riches of other nations, are a burden to us; the land is not improv'd, the product is not manufactur'd; the fishing and other advantages for foreign trade are neglected: and the reason generally given is, that laziness and want of honesty are natural to us.

If want of honesty and laziness were natural, they would be so to mankind; or if peculiar to a people, this would be so to the Dutch rather than to us: the air of Holland is grosser which inclines to laziness; and the country not producing wherewith to maintain the inhabitants, would force them to rob or cheat their neighbours, or one another. But it is more reasonable to think laziness and want of honesty are vices, the consequences of poverty; and poverty the consequence of a faulty administration. If the same measures had been taken in Scotland for encouraging trade, as was taken in Holland, we had been a more powerful and richer nation than Holland. If Spain, France and Britain, or any one of them had apply'd to trade, as early, and upon the same measures Holland did; Holland would not have been inhabited. But by their early application, and the wrong measures of other countries, they have got such great magazines of what's necessary for their maintenance and defence; of rich commodities to sell to other nations, of materials for shipping, &c. and such a quantity of silver, esteem'd above its value as a metal by being used as money: that in all appearance so long as silver is used as money, the great quantity they have of it, with their great oeconomy, enabling them to under-sell other nations; they will maintain the rank they hold in trade, and consequently in power; notwithstanding their natural disadvantages, the present application, and natural advantages of other nations.

This country is more capable of an extended trade than

any other country of Europe, yet it is reduc'd to a very low state. Trade is ruin'd; the national stock is wasted; the people forsake the country; the rents of land are unpay'd; houses in towns, and farms in the country are thrown upon the owners hands; the creditor cannot have the interest of his money to live upon; and the debitor's person and estate are expos'd to the law.

The landed man, by having engaged his person and estate for the payment of a species, which is not in his power to perform; and having no alternative: by the law his person is at the mercy of the creditor, and his estate to be sold for so much of that species as it will yield. If 2 or 3 money'd men call in their money, with a design to force their debitors to part with their estates, at what prices they please to impose: they may bring the price of land to 15 or 10 years purchase. For they would not take bonds in payment, and few or none would be in a condition to buy with money.

If victual should prove scarce, as we have not goods or money for any value to send out for corns; so only a part of the people could be maintained: the better part would have bread, but the more necessary part, the labouring men, would be forc'd to leave the country, or to starve in it. Nor would they fare better in England; for as the scarcity of money has set idle many of the people of England, so there are more already than there is employment for: and our people, at least many of them, would meet the same fate they had endeavoured to evite.

The landed men would want people to labour the ground; they would perhaps get food and cloathing for themselves and families, but these they were owing to, in all appearance, would get nothing: for the case being general, and the landed men the stronger party; they would not suffer their liberty and estates to be taken from them. But tho' the law could be put in execution, and the estates of the landed men were put to sale; as there would be few purchasers, the price of land would fall very low.

Suppose the land were sold or given among the creditors for 15 years purchase, or less; it would be sold for more than it were worth, for they would not find people to labour it: so many would be sufferers, and none gainers.

If neither of these cases happen; yet this country cannot well subsist in the condition 'tis in: if this opportunity is neglected, if wrong or ineffectual measures are taken, in all appearance we will be in confusion before we have another opportunity.

To raise or allay the money, to coin the plate, or regulate trade, are offer'd as measures to supply the want of money: and 'tis thought any one of them will bring us out of our difficulties. When they come to be examin'd, raising or allaying the money will be found no help but a hurt to the country, whatever our circumstances are. The others may prove ineffectual.

'Tis thought our import and expence abroad this last year exceeded our export by a very considerable sum, so to make the ballance equal, we must not only retrench equal to the money which was sent out last year; but likeways so much more as the want of that money, and of the addition the bank made to our money may have lessen'd the yearly value. So tho' 'tis possible that coining the plate and regulating trade may bring the ballance to our side, yet 'tis to be fear'd the consequences will show that it is not very practicable; for that and other reasons already given. However they may assist, but in regulating our import, regard ought to be had that the sale of our goods abroad be no way hindred, for if that is not taken care of, we shall lose more for want of a market, than we shall save by importing less. And tho' all necessary care be taken, yet the assistance may reasonably be expected from these measures, will not relieve us; they may keep us lingring in the state we are, expos'd to confusion at home, and to insults from abroad.

Most people think scarcity of money is only the

consequence of a ballance due; but 'tis the cause as well as the consequence, and the effectual way to bring the ballance to our side, is to add to the money.

Our poor have been computed 200000, our people were then more than now, but our poor may be as many as then; suppose only 100000, and by the addition to our money 50000 of them were imployed, and only for one half of the year, their labour to be payed 3 pence, and worth 3 pence more to the imployer, their consumption a penny more than now: the yearly value of the nation would be increas'd by such labour 189583 lib. 6 sh. and 8 pence.

If the country people about Perth and Stirling, have to the value of 20000 lib. of linen, serges, and other manufacture more than is bought up; tho' these goods exported will yield 20 or 30 per cent. profit, yet the owners can't export them, the goods being in so many different hands, and not having correspondents abroad to whom they could trust the sale of them. A. B. and C. are satisfied for that profit to take the trouble and hazard of exporting them, but money being scarce they cannot get any to borrow, tho' their security be good; nor cannot well have credit for the goods from so many different people they are strangers to. If they could have credit for them, yet these country people must be idle till A. B. and C. pay them out of their returns from abroad. So for want of money to exchange by, goods fall in value, and manufacture decays.

It cannot well be known, what sum will serve the occasions of the nation, for as manufacture and trade advance, the demand for money will increase; but the many poor we have always had, is a great presumption we have never had money enough.

England has been computed to have had 14 millions in gold and silver, and at the same time had paper money for a great sum; yet England never had money enough to imploy the people: 50 million would not improve England so far as it is capable of improvement. If all the people were then imployed and to the best advantage, more money would bring more people from other countries. The province of Holland by a great quantity of money, and numbers of people the consequence of much money, is able to bear a share in the wars of Europe, equal to many times the same number of acres of better land in England; yet Holland has not the advantages for trade that England has. So that country that can have money equal to the demand, will be more powerful than any other country with the same advantages, whose money is less than the demand.

If money were given to a people in greater quantity than there was a demand for, money would fall in its value; but if only given equal to the demand, it will not fall in value.

At present perhaps 3 or 400000 lib. is more than there is a demand for, but as trade and manufacture increase, the demand for money will be greater.

What I have propos'd to supply the country with money, may be reduc'd to this. If an estate of a 100 lib. rent is worth 2000 lib. in silver-money, and this estate can be convey'd by paper, and this paper be capable of being divided; then that estate may be made current money for 2000 lib. and any person who receives such paper money, receives a value equal to the same sum of silver money, as silver is valued now. If it is coin'd for 15 years purchase, then that paper-money will be more valuable than silver, for 1500 lib. in that paper will purchase land worth 2000 lib. silver-money. If it is coin'd for 25 years purchase, then that paper money will not be as valuable as silver, for 2000 lib. in silver will buy as much land as 2500 lib. in paper.

Since it is very practicable to make land money, it would be contrary to reason to limit the industry of the people, by making it depend on a species that is not in our power, but in the power of our enemies; when we have a species of our own every way more qualified.

And considering the state of this country from the great scarcity of money; that the value of lands fall, rents are unpayed, farms are thrown upon the master's hand, and the debitor's person and estate expos'd to the law, being engag'd to pay a species of which there is scarce any in the nation.

2. The hazard the money'd man is in from the uncertainty of the value of money, and the danger of confusion, in which case the money'd man may lose all.

3. The low state of trade, that many of the people who depended on trade and liv'd well, are starving or forc'd abroad.

4. That the other degrees of the people suffer in proportion.

5. That the nation in this condition may run into confusion, and is expos'd to its enemies.

Considering the benefit the nation will have by this addition to the money; that the land will be improv'd, so be more valuable, rents be well payed, and that debitors by paying a value equal to what is contracted for, may free their persons and estates from the danger they are now exposed to.

2. That the money'd man will receive punctual payment, in a money of a more certain value than silver, or any other goods, and be in no danger of confusion.

3. That trade will flourish, and these who depend on it will be encouraged.

4. That the condition of the other degrees of the people will be better'd.

5. That the nation will be able to maintain itself in order, and resist its enemies.

These reasons considered, the question then will be, whether we will improve the country as much as it is capable without being at any expence for a measure of trade, or continue as we are in hopes of silver from other nations.

It will be a great advantage to this nation, that by the register we are capable of putting this proposal in execution, and enjoying the benefit of it, when other nations, tho' they resolv'd upon it, would for some years be incapable of it. Tho' for the general good of Europe it were to be wish'd England were as capable of it as we are.

I have not had time to put my thoughts in that order they ought to have been, and am forc'd to leave out answers I design'd to have given to some objections I have heard made against this proposal; but if the parliament think good to enter upon the consideration of it, I don't doubt but it may be made appear to be of great and certain advantage that it cannot possibly be any way hurtful to the country in general, and that it may be so ordered, as not to be hurtful to any person, but on the contrair.

FINIS.

GLOSSARY

Some of the words and phrases used in Money and Trade Considered have either not made their way into modern English, or are so seldom used that they are unfamiliar enough to require explanation.

Accompt:
Account.

Agio:
The variations from fixed pars or rates of exchange in the currencies of different countries.

Boll:
Dry measure of weight or capacity. It was abolished in Scotland in 1879 by the introduction of imperial weights and measures.

Britannia Languens:
Short form description of the economic text *Britannia languens, or a Discourse of Trade Shewing the Grounds and Reasons of the Increase and Decay of Land-rents, National Wealth and Strength: With Application to the Late and Present State and Condition of England, France, and the United Provinces*, by William Petyt, first published in 1680.

Chalder:

Scottish measure of oats.

Denier:

French unit of currency equal in value to one sol.

Dispone:

To convey legal title or authority to another.

Dollar:

Scottish unit of currency equal in value to sixty Scottish shillings.

Drawback:

Import duties or taxes repaid by a government, in whole or in part, when the imported goods are exported or used in the manufacture of exported goods.

Drug:

An unsalable commodity, or one for which there is no demand.

Ducat/Ducatdown:

A widely used unit of currency equal in value to forty shillings; issued by various countries in Europe including Scotland and The Netherlands.

Duit:

Dutch unit of currency equal in value to one-eighth of a stiver/stuiver.

Fashion:

To forge or counterfeit. The process of making, forming, giving shape to.

Fiars:

Scottish legal expression given to the prices of grain determined by the sheriffs in the various counties assisted by juries.

Firlot:
Scottish dry measure equal to one-quater of a boll.

First Cost:
The cost of something calculated by adding the cost of materials used to make it and the cost of paying somebody to make it, but not including costs that are connected with running a business, such as rent and electricity.

Ell:
French unit of length equal to fifty-four inches.

Groat:
Scottish unit of currency equal in value to four pence.

Guilder/Gulden:
Dutch unit of currency equal in value to twenty stivers.

Guinea:
English unit of currency equal in value to one pound or twenty shillings, but with the fluctuation in the price of gold, had been known to reach thirty shillings.

Landwart:
Countryside.

Livre:
French unit of currency equal in value to twenty sols.

Locke, Mr:
John Locke, English philosopher (1632-1704).

Louis d'or:
French unit of currency of fluctuating value.

Magazine:
A place in which goods are stored; or the contents of such a place.

Mark:
See Merk.

Martinmass/Martinmas:

Saint Martin's Day, a church festival held on the 11th of November.

Merk/Mark:

Scottish unit of currency equal in value to thirteen shillings and four pence.

Mun, Mr.:

Thomas Mun, English economist (1571-1641).

Overplus:

Surplus.

Petty, Sir William:

English economist (1623-1687).

Plack:

Scottish unit of currency equal in value to one-twelfth of an English penny.

Plate:

A piece of metal on which anything is engraved for the purpose of being printed; hence, an impression from the engraved metal.

Rochel:

Wine imported from the port of La Rochelle, France.

Serges:

A twilled wollen fabric.

Sol:

French unit of currency equal in value to one-twentieth of a livre.

Sous:

See Sol.

Stiver:

Dutch unit of currency equal in value to eight duiten.

Tun/Tunn:

A cask holding the equivalent of 954 litres of wine.

Vent:

The sale or exchange of commodities.

Victual:

Food fit for human consumption. Used in this book to describe a common method of rent payable by a tenant farmer to a land owner.

Victualling:

Supplying with food fit for human consumption.

Wadset:

The conveyance of land in pledge for a debt. A form of mortgage, exchanging the use of lands for the loan of a capital sum, subject to reversion.

Whitsunday:

One of the Scottish quater-days falling on the 15th of May.

Years Purchase:

The amount yielded by the annual income of property. Used to express the value of a thing in the number of years required for its income to yield its purchase price.

ALSO AVAILABLE FROM NEWTON PAGE

Newton Page books are available at all good bookstores and online book retailers. For more information about our books and how to order them, please visit our website:

www.newtonpage.com

ALSO AVAILABLE FROM NEWTON PAGE

John Law of Lauriston

Financier and Statesman, Founder of the Bank of France, Originator of the Mississippi Scheme

A. W. Wiston-Glynn

ISBN-13: 978-1934619032

The true story of a Scottish murderer, philanderer, gambler and abscondee who escaped his condemned cell in London to become the darling of the French economy, John Law of Lauriston is an account of the euphoria and wealth Law created by engineering the first stock market boom, and the despair, poverty and destruction which followed its inevitable crash.

Newton Page books are available at all good bookstores and online book retailers. For more information about our books and how to order them, please visit our website:

www.newtonpage.com

ALSO AVAILABLE FROM NEWTON PAGE

The Mississippi Bubble

A Memoir of John Law

Adolphe Thiers

ISBN-13: 978-1934619056

An established classic and authoritative historical analysis of the spectacular rise and fall of the most enigmatic genius in financial and economic history. It provides a compelling biographical narrative of John Law's life, a considered examination of his Mississippi Scheme, and enlightening accounts of both the Darien Expedition and South Sea Bubble.

Newton Page books are available at all good bookstores and online book retailers. For more information about our books and how to order them, please visit our website:

www.newtonpage.com

ALSO AVAILABLE FROM NEWTON PAGE

The Life of John Law

Including a Detailed Account of the Rise,
Progress and Termination of the Mississippi System

John Phillip Wood

ISBN-13: 978-1934619018

One of the most cited biographies of John Law in existence. It is both a concise and gripping retelling of the extraordinary life story of the 'first millionaire' and also a very readable and entertaining account of the remarkably swift rise and even swifter decline of both of his influential innovations: the Mississippi Company and the Mississippi Scheme.

Newton Page books are available at all good bookstores and online book retailers. For more information about our books and how to order them, please visit our website:

www.newtonpage.com

ALSO AVAILABLE FROM NEWTON PAGE

The Financier Law

His Scheme and Times: A Graphic Description of the Origin, Maturity and Wreck of the Mississippi Scheme

André Cochut

ISBN-13: 978-1934619049

A richly contextual narrative of the life of John Law, a charismatic Scottish economist and murderer and who would escape execution and use his seemingly effortless financial genius to rise from obscurity to become the most powerful member of the French court, the controller of the French economy, and the richest man the modern world had ever seen.

Newton Page books are available at all good bookstores and online book retailers. For more information about our books and how to order them, please visit our website:

www.newtonpage.com

ALSO AVAILABLE FROM NEWTON PAGE

Letters to John Law

A Letter to Mr. Law
The Case of Mr. Law Truly Stated
A Second Letter to Mr. Law

Selected and introduced by

Gavin John Adams

ISBN-13: 978-1-934619087

This collection of three uncompromising early eighteenth-century propagandist pamphlets documents the wildly contrasting reactions to Law's surprise return to Britain. Crafted by the most prominent journalists, commentators and political agitators of the day, each provides an invaluable contemporaneous social, political and historical record of the most remarkable story in financial history.

Newton Page books are available at all good bookstores and online book retailers. For more information about our books and how to order them, please visit our website:

www.newtonpage.com

ALSO AVAILABLE FROM NEWTON PAGE

John Law and the Mississippi Scheme

The Chimera (1720)
The Case of Mr. Law Truly Stated (1721)
Selected Journalism (1719-1722)

Daniel Defoe

ISBN-13: 978-1-934619070

Daniel Defoe is the father of economic and financial journalism. This anthology is testament to his remarkable insight into the European economic crises of the 1720s. His contemporary accounts of the euphoria and excesses of the first ever stock market boom unleashed by John Law and his Mississippi Scheme, and the despair and poverty that followed its crash betray a chilling prescience and an unyielding strength of conviction that very few journalists have possessed since

Newton Page books are available at all good bookstores and online book retailers. For more information about our books and how to order them, please visit our website:

www.newtonpage.com

Printed in Great Britain
by Amazon